The World of
Children

The World of Children

CONTRIBUTORS: Philippe Ariès   Edward Blishen   Phyllis Hostler   Dan Jacobson
Marghanita Laski   Colin MacInnes   Alastair Reid   Anthony Storr   Elizabeth Taylor   Anthony Thwaite

special sequences photographed by Michael Joseph

Paul Hamlyn · London

Published by Paul Hamlyn Ltd
Drury House · Russell Street · London WC2
Literary editor: Edward Blishen
Executive editor: Joan Clibbon, Art Director: Felix Brenner
Text editors: Hazel Westbury, Linda Oberholtz
Picture editor: Ronald Setter
Designer: Patrick Coyle
© Copyright 1966 Paul Hamlyn Ltd

Phototypeset in 11 on 12 pt Imprint by Oliver Burridge Filmsetting Ltd, England
Printed in Italy—Officine Grafiche A. Mondadori—Verona

Contents

Publisher's preface

We have all had the same experience: sitting, perhaps, in a crowded train, and looking around at faces—lined, heavy, sunken or sad—we have all thought with wonder: '*All these people—and myself—were children once.*'

This book has been created, in part, as a celebration of the sense of wonder grown-ups often feel as they watch the very young, or look back to the pangs and pleasures of being young themselves. It shows children engrossed in exploring their environment. Their attention is fixed in a dozen ways on the absorbing business of living. Everything is being discovered for the first time: parents, people in general, words, colours, shadows—even their own shapes. In many of the pictures we have collected here, the sheer beauty of children—the loveliness of their gestures, their grace and evident joy—is captured. A small girl who is photographed racing towards the sea— a bird with her arms outstretched—delights the heart and the eye.

But the aim was to do more than celebrate the beauty of childhood. These children are poor as well as rich, happy as well as unhappy, safe and in danger—children of all colours and many creeds, their hopes in life resting on a wide variety of political, economic and social situations. The prevailing attitude today is one of deep pessimism about the hostilities that divide our world. But the pictures and text in this book provide a strong and cheering sense of how similar all children are. The qualities that they seem to share everywhere, especially eagerness for life, are a heartening reminder of how many attractive qualities men possess, and of how much, wherever they live, they have in common.

The book begins at the moment when the child is born. It ends with children at that strange point in their lives when they are hovering on the brink of adolescence. Between the two there is an enormous distance. For most children the journey takes perhaps thirteen years, but these years are longer and infinitely more crowded than any others in the human span. This book tries to map that journey with both photographs and essays. The photographs were collected over a period of years from all over the world.

The writers who chronicle the child's progress from birth are well-known English novelists, poets, teachers. One is a noted psychiatrist. Their problem (and ours) was how to divide up the essentially indivisible experience of childhood so that the milestones and crises of growing up could best be presented and observed. Though some of the contributors have drawn on their knowledge of modern psychology, the book is far from a technical treatise. Most contributors tapped their own private memories of childhood and their experiences as parents. Their aim is to throw as imaginative and sensitive a light as possible on the nature of childhood. All of them have tried to avoid the easy danger of lapsing into sentimentality. (One writer, Marghanita Laski, reminds us, looking back into history, that society has not always felt a special compassion for the young.)

Growing up has always been a full-time job—which really requires a lifetime. It does not seem to have become any easier as the world grows older and more complex. Each man's beginnings, though, are always full of high promise.

Prologue

Elizabeth Taylor

For an adult to be told he is behaving childishly, is to heap shame upon him: as we heap shame on children by calling them babyish. ('Childlike', for some reason, is a different matter. This implies spiritual qualities—childlike faith and childlike wonder, for instance.)

I have attempted to see as a whole this state we have grown out of—or should have grown out of. Did all the aspects of it, written about in this book, give me a general view of childhood? I closed my eyes and tried to see the picture which the word 'child' formed in my mind—a rather solitary, Wordsworthian Little Maid it was, or perhaps more like Beatrix Potter's Lucy, living in the country, of course, but preferably the *seaside*-country, so that she could see a World in a Grain of Sand and a Heaven in a Wild Flower all at the same time. Then a real child, whooping through the garden, shattered the vision by seeming so much more interesting, so that he was himself first and child later, if one bothered to classify him at all. He had once won his way into my heart by asking me to open a jar of sweets for him, because 'old wrinkled hands get a better grip'.

Well, that's one thing we've grown out of—unheeding honesty. We don't ask our older relations if we can have certain things when they die, as I have been by my younger relations. We leave a lot of thoughts resting in our heads.

To children, I think that thoughts come as sudden flashes against a background of musing—a kind of bee's-droning, hypnotic trance. They rattle a stick along the railings, their eyes are glazed and their lips move in a wordless chant—and then they are suddenly riveted, something catches their attention and opens wide the veiled eyes and the stick is thrown away. The outside world has made its claim.

It is certain that time is elastic to young children. There can be agonies of fidgety irritation, when five minutes seems forever, and other occasions when time literally does cease to exist, as it never will again in later life. I remember—perhaps I was six years old—going to school one afternoon alone. It must have been in early autumn, for all up the avenue I had to climb there were beech-nuts lying round the boles of the trees. I began to collect them—some three-sided, plump and glossy, others flat and empty. I peeled and ate them and filled the front pockets of my satchel. Then a large white convolvulus high on a hedge caught my attention, and I reached to pick it. Almost at once, in the sun, it closed up and was not wonderful any more. And so I meandered on. I was utterly astonished when I arrived at school to find that it was the end of the last lesson. All I had seemed to do was to walk to school as usual. I was made to stand in a corner until the bell rang, while the class shuffled and stared in awed, self-righteous wonder. They were glad of the diversion, as at school one was glad of any diversion—such as the delightful morning when the music-teacher fainted at prayers, going down with a slither and a wallop in a quite fascinating way. Another time, sudden snow made a diversion. There was an excuse to stay at home from school, but I was not to be left out of anything, and was rewarded by the strangeness of school with few children there, and a different, more muffled sound, and a new light on the high ceiling from all the whiteness outside; and I remember it clearly after more than forty years. That day of disrupted routine was better than a holiday.

Time is elastic, and weather only matters in its extremes. It has to affect a child with really great discomfort before it is noticed. I can feel now, in my imagination, the pain of frost in my fingertips, and my mother gradually thawing them out in a bowl to which she kept adding more and more hot water. I had stayed too long playing outside—some game in which leaves were not leaves, but other companions, with whom I had been having bossy conversations. The bitter fact of the cold impinged too late on me, and there was the sudden consciousness of pain, and the broken and abandoned game.

Apart from discomfort, the weather might be noticed if it were likely to upset arrangements, and then the sky would be watched with a mariner's eye lest the river-picnic would have to be cancelled. And often one desired rain so passionately that one felt quite ill with the intensity of trying to will it out of the clouds—so that some dreaded outing might be postponed, some terrible treat which had been arranged for one's pleasure: one of those excursions grown-ups imagine that children enjoy—especially visits to other unknown children.

I suppose that the chief thing about being a child is being in the power of grown-ups. Everything comes from them—food, laws, treats and punishments. They have the power to give or to withhold. Some of them make up the rules as they go along to suit their convenience and the child, who would like the chance to make up a few rules himself, knows it.

Children are afraid when they do not know what will happen next, or else have an inkling and a dread and can do nothing. I once wrote about a little boy leaving hospital with his mother after a tonsillectomy. He says, on the way home, 'I was afraid all the time of what they would do to me next, but I got out before they could do the worst thing of all.'

'What would the worst thing be?'

'I kept hearing them say I would have to have my bowels opened.'

It was a true thing that had been said to *me*, and made me realize the abyss of terror into which children are thrown by careless and misunderstood words. They brood and feel, superstitiously, that to ask for an explanation will make the horror real at once.

This was a completely thoughtless piece of silliness on the part of grown-ups—the failure to explain: but there are also all the calculated rudenesses to perplex children, to keep them in the fog—the French talked over their heads or, earlier, the words spelled out. 'I'm afraid he's rather t-i-r-e-d.' And what, for heaven's sake, does this 't-i-r-e-d' mean that he mustn't know about? Perhaps he is going to die of it, since they dare not let him know.

Do parents forget, or do they consciously reverse their opinions, so that now they truly believe that Mother and Father know best? The well-known miseries of the great plateful of food over which they themselves must have sighed and gagged, stirring their tears into the cold rice-pudding—it seems that this memory has altogether faded, and a virtue has been made out of the suffering. There were itchy vests, too, in the past, and conspicuous garments, which drew unwanted attention; there was the fear of being laughed at, or having one's parents laughed at. All forgotten. Hardly a

'. . . a real child, whooping through the garden . . .'

lesson learnt.

Social strain is such an affliction of childhood—from baby-hood, even. 'Give Grandma a lovely smile.' Then 'Kiss Uncle goodbye.' Then 'Come and say "how-d'you-do" to every-one.' ('No, he's not really shy. He's just being silly.')

If only one could have been allowed to be spontaneous—to fling one's arms around Uncle—or not. To open one's birthday presents in secret, to gloat over them or be dis-appointed privately, without the adults watching one's face for expressions of joy. How delightful and impossible! It was so tiring all that reacting to them; but the price one had to pay. And it was good training, perhaps, for the insincerities of later life.

It is no wonder that among themselves young children allow themselves to be simpler. They show their motives with the most delightful frankness. Two little boys each had a sweet. I heard one say, 'Aren't you going to eat yours?' and the other replied, 'No, I'm leaving it for when you haven't got one.'

Of course, the suffering is not all on one side in the relation-ship between children and adults. The young have an eroding effect. They, too, can be thick-headed, so may parents be vulnerable; for they are not in the least like the idealized mothers and fathers in the books written (by other grown-ups, of course) for children—those Mrs Darlings, whose likeness never was on land or sea.

I often wonder how children measure their own, ordinary mothers against such a pattern of perfection. Perhaps it does not occur to them to do so; but such ideas occur to me as I, rather shamefacedly, read the stories aloud.

Some of the mothers seem to have been so saintly, so beautiful, so gentle that they were impossible to describe or bring to life, and so are dead before the book begins.

I am irritated. I would like to write a children's book about the kind of mother I was myself—weak, so often at the end of my tether, liable to sudden exasperations, sudden spoilings, empty threats, boredoms with the young; and, patience finally worn away, longings to skip off and leave them for a while. Nothing was cut and dried, and I don't suppose they knew where they were—my children. There were the vacillations about whether they were really not well enough to go to school or 'crying wolf'. How to tell? I almost spun a coin. And the coin, knowing no more than I did, often came down wrong. By half-past ten, the child was either tearing madly round the house in the pink of condition, or I was on my way to the school to fetch him back because of his sudden rise in temperature. I cannot recall any mother in those books for children who would have made such mistakes. 'I'm not an example. I'm a warning,' I often said in self-defence. My grown-up daughter said to me recently, 'One thing I was grateful to you for was that you always gave me a choice of punishments.' More uncertainties and vacillations, I thought.

One of the things one can be surest of with children is their love of ritual and repetition—the same old story that they know by heart, the same games played in the same way, the same pattern of Christmas and birthday. They love to know the way things are going, and pleasures repeated are intensi-fied. There is none of that superstitious feeling that grown

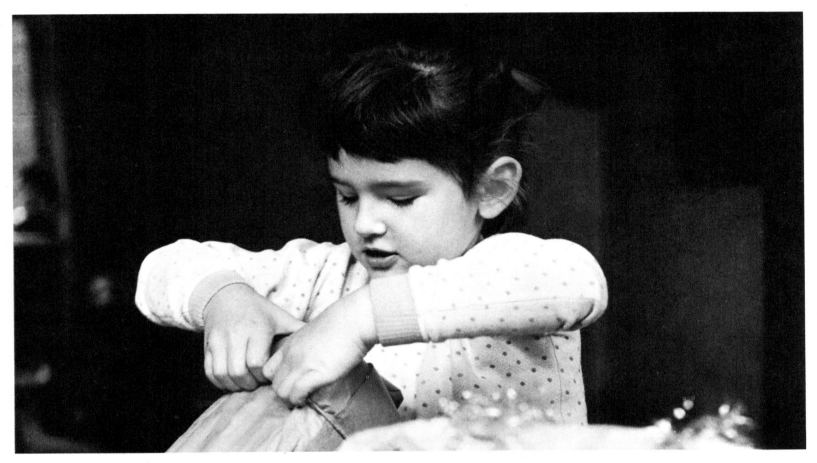

people have of 'never going back'.

One little boy we fetch from London to stay with us every holiday, gets into the car, and before we have driven out of his street, he leans over my husband's seat and says, 'Go on, sing that song.' Farther on, my husband must stop to buy me a bunch of flowers at a certain spot, because once he did. And as soon as he reaches our house, the child goes to a cupboard, and puts on an enormous pair of old Wellington boots, in which he slops happily and familiarly about. He remembers his own beaker and his own place at the table, and he picks up the family phrases again, as if they have never been off his lips. But I wait for the day, when he will suddenly say, 'Why do you always buy the flowers at *that* place?' or 'Why must I always sit here with my back to the window?' For many years, whenever my husband drove through a certain railway-tunnel the children clamoured for him to blow the horn, loving its echo. He came to do it automatically, and went on doing so too long. 'Why on earth do you always do that?' he was one day asked.

Make believe is the child's prerogative—a thing we must grow out of for our own comfort and that of everybody else. When we are older, we must see things for what they are; but a child scarcely ever does. To him, an old log becomes a hobby-horse and the real hobby-horse is thrown into a pond to be a raft for ship-wrecked sailors to cling to. I have seen a little boy, completely absorbed, on tip-toe, using a hollyhock as a telephone. Cats and dogs are dressed up as dolls, and dolls become children. Imagination makes magic come about, with murmured impersonations and firmness. For once, the child is in power over his environment. One can learn a lot about the grown-ups in his life by watching him. I have a sly delight in doing that. It is akin to the heady pleasure of seeing other people's children behaving badly at, for instance, those nursery tea-parties when one leant over chairs offering choco-late cake, or made a circle for *The Farmer's in the Dell*. How graciously one could afford to make excuses for some other little creature's tantrums. Unfortunately, it wasn't always that way round, and one tried to tell oneself that in this life one must give as well as take, and that on this occasion it was someone else's turn to be gracious.

Making scenes. I love this expression for it is exactly what happens. I remember taking my very young children to a museum where there was a skeleton in a glass case. My little girl backed away in horror. 'It's nothing,' her bigger brother said. '*You're* like that inside.' She howled so loudly that people turned to stare, frowning at Mother, as they always do—as if I had just twisted her wrist. 'For Heaven's sake, what's wrong?' I asked. 'He's just been dreadfully rude to me,' she cried, casting herself about on the floor. It was a day of shame. (So many were.) At the exit, I put a coin into a collecting-box. 'Why did you do that?' my son inquired loudly. 'They ask for help in keeping the museum going,' I explained. 'Threepence won't help much,' he said coolly. And heads were turned aside, to hide smiles; mine was turned aside for a different reason.

Shame is a wasted and negative emotion; but between parents and children it crops up all the time.

Going to bed—the attitude towards it—is a thing which

sharply divides the child from the adult. To a child, it is associated with the thought of games abruptly broken off, with being solitary and bored; often with punishment; often with fear. I remember the long evenings in summer, lying restlessly in bed, listening to the voices of older, or luckier children still playing out-of-doors, and I would creep softly across to the window and lean out, dreaming, watching clouds and gnats, or a spider making a web, to be brought back with utter shock, by the stern voice in the room behind me.

Yet, bad as summer was, winter was much worse. Darkness was dreadful. 'Shut the door after you. Must you always be told?' Yes, I must always be told; for whatever was said, however exasperated *they* became, I should try it every night. For I was afraid to cut off their voices, and go upstairs alone, and also afraid to tell them I was afraid. 'Goodnight,' I would shout on every stair, and across the dimly lighted landing—which I thought was made for ghosts—trying to keep in contact. And there was such silence up there. Sometimes, a door downstairs would suddenly burst open, and let out a gust of laughter and chatter. I was glad of it, callous as it sounded. Up there in my solitude, I was alone with spectres and the prospect of nightmares. At this time, I must have been too old for anyone to imagine such timidity in me. I was old enough to be *sent* to bed, not *put*. Some of the dreams certainly were bad—crowded with sinister figures. These nightmares were usually in black and white. I would wake with relief, and will myself to keep awake until it was morning. The beautiful dreams were in beautiful colours—the meadows of Persephone, without the horror, which was a very real one to me as a child. Those lovely blue and green and golden dreams—they seemed to make blissful all of the next day.

I remember going one morning to wake up my daughter when she was very small. She opened her eyes and said, 'Put your head on the pillow quickly and get the rest of my lovely dream.' She knew that the magic must fade, but it still seemed to shine all about her, to be *in* that room, so that I could catch a glimpse if I were quick enough.

There was so much magic in childhood—the snow came, and spellbound the whole of one's world; fog cast its own spell too. I loved fog. It made the most ordinary things very mysterious.

There was also magic one had to deal with oneself—staving it off, or bringing it about, according to whether it was benign or not. Count the railings carefully, touch each one, there might be a lion behind them; don't step on the crack between the paving-stones or the earth might open up as it did for poor Persephone. I tried also to bring off magic myself—not only being a rain-maker, but once—after being taken to see *Peter Pan*—trying to fly. I was so taken with the idea of it that I felt sure it was possible. That very night I made my attempt. I opened the bedroom window wide, to allow for my passage through it. I felt elated, as light as air. I balanced on the end of my bed, and imagined the rooftops, the stars, I raised my arms, launched myself, and crashed.

Which in a way brings me to Faith with a capital 'F'. My husband had had a similar experience to mine; but being a more religious child, *he* had tried walking on the water, and with not a doubt in his head that he could do so.

Religion made only fleeting impressions on me. I was once taken to Sunday School, but screamed so loudly that I was quickly taken home again, and that was the end of that. At kindergarten, I puzzled vaguely about the incomprehensible hymns—all that fuss about the green hill just because it had no city wall. And what on earth did *Hallelujah* mean? It had a very jeering ring about it to me. Then, we should plough the fields—and at once apparently rush off in all directions, like people who have fused time-bombs. 'God's Almighty Hand' was alarming. There was obviously not a chance against *that*. What a fearsome picture to lie in bed on a long summer's evening and think about. Can that be the childlike faith that is so much respected?

I remember praying—'Please God, do not appear to me in a vision.' And I hoped He would not take offence—as so many of the Greek gods and goddesses (who were just as real to me) were prone to do. I would try to propitiate the lot. They seemed so touchy.

There were other horrors connected with God. Up There —where He sat on the highest cloud—all the dead were vaguely floating about; but not so vaguely that they hadn't an ear or an eye for what was going on on earth—shameful things, too, like the picking of noses and the telling of lies. They were malign—the dead. They were like the grown-ups, ranged against oneself, *and* with inside information. It never occurred to me then that they might understand what the living could not, or see one's good intentions for what they were. And it does not occur to me now.

On Good Fridays, I recoiled in horror. I could not bear this going over and over such a terrible story. There was the burden of guilt, too. 'I didn't want that poor man to do that for *me*.' It was done, too, to make me good, and it hadn't worked. I tried to put it out of my mind.

I said my prayers at night: but only because I daren't risk not saying them; in the same way as I touched the railings and skipped over the paving-cracks. To say them was a small, if irksome, insurance.

Ivy Compton-Burnett, who, I think, writes better about children than anyone ever has, has a beautiful thing to say about children's prayers in *Darkness and Day*. Two little girls are getting into bed.

'You have not said your prayers,' said Fanshawe, when they had lain down.

'No,' said Rose, in agreement.

'You may say them in bed tonight. But think what you are saying, and don't miss out anything.'

Rose put her hands to her face, as the door closed.

'May I be forgiven and saved,' she said.

'May I be forgiven and saved,' said Viola, with a perfunctory similar movement. *'It was a good idea, wasn't it?'*

'Yes, it takes in everything. Nothing else is needed. What is the good of a long prayer or a hymn? They are just wasted.'

'Wouldn't it do just to say, "May I be saved?"'

'No, we ought to show a feeling of sin. We must not think only of our own side.'

'Not when the other side is God's,' said Viola, with reverence.

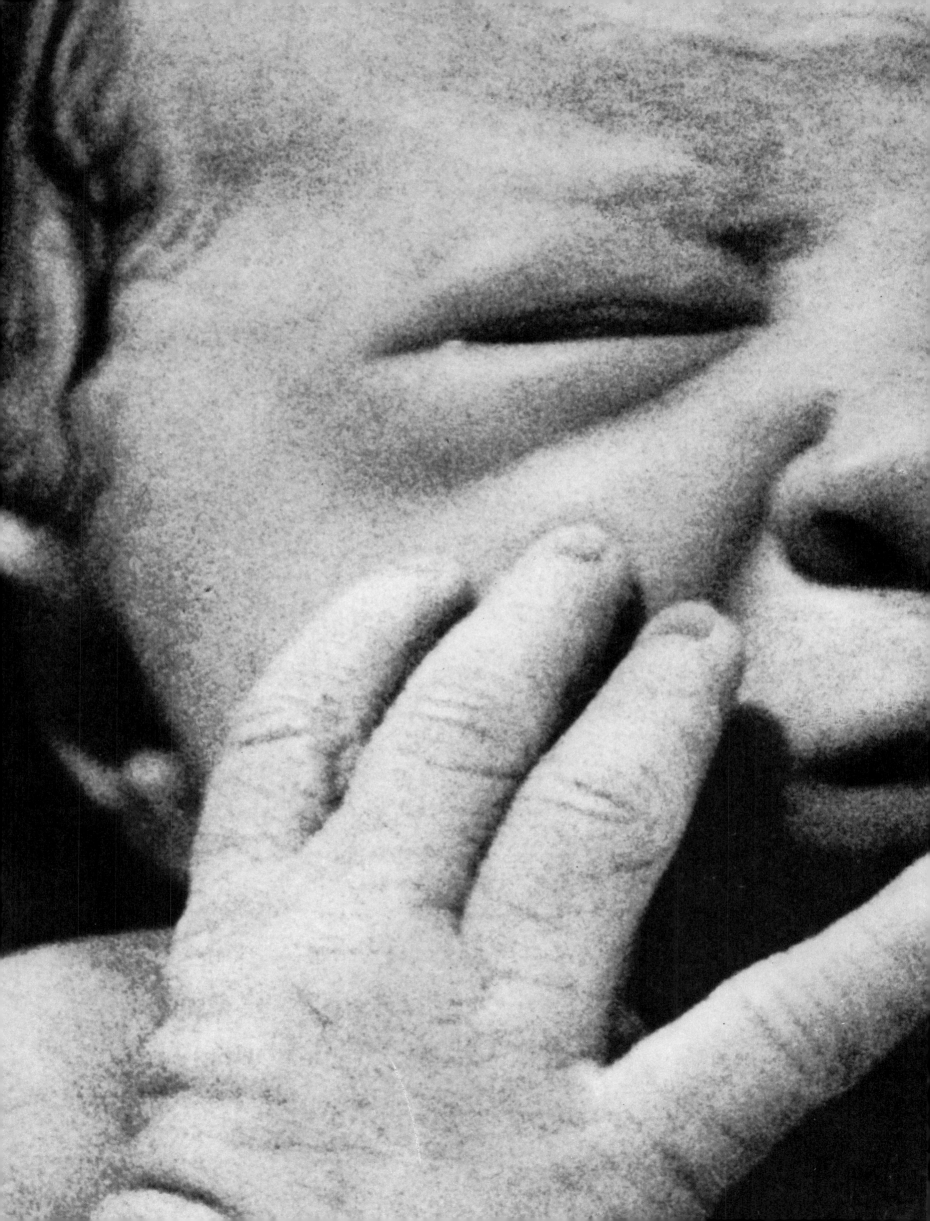

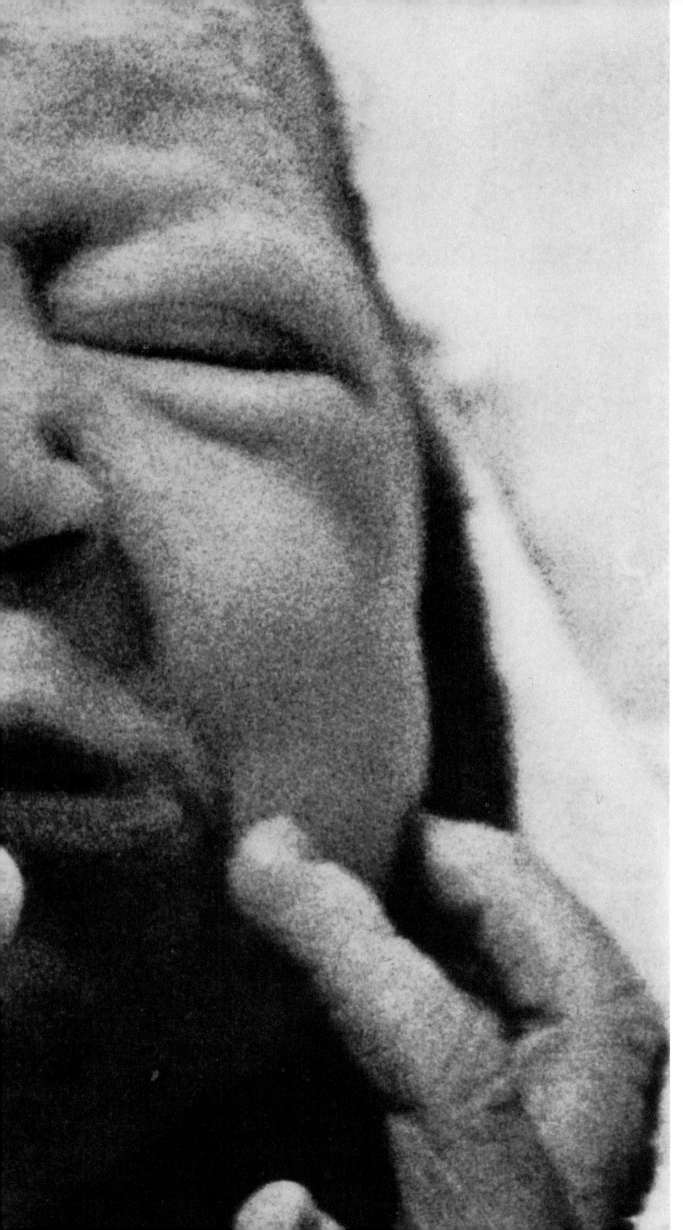

Beginnings

Still damp, its skin still wrinkled from the sea it has lived in so long, the wizened, ancient face of a new born baby is in many ways a terrifying sight. For one thing, even though 125 million babies are born every year, most people in their lifetime never actually see a baby just after it has been taken from the womb. Human dignity is a delicately maintained illusion. The unexpected sight of a new born baby is a shock to it.

It is not unfamiliarity alone that troubles the observer but a brooding sense of the infinity of time, and the small moment of any human life. In its mother's womb the development of its eyes, hands and brain has miraculously re-traced the course of their evolution in the entire human species—from the fish of 400 million years ago that first acquired eyes, from the preprimates of fifty million years ago that first learned to manipulate their hands.

Perhaps because of this slowly acquired complexity, human babies, after birth, are the slowest earthly creatures to reach growth. A human child takes over twenty years to mature, and during most of that time it needs protection not required by any other animal. Today, psychologists, neurologists and biologists are busy trying to assess babies' brains and bodies, as well as their consciousness. Science has brought us much new knowledge so that today, as never before, the importance of a child's experiences in his beginnings is generally appreciated, if not fully understood. In the following essay author Anthony Storr, a practising psychiatrist and a practising father as well, tries to explore the world of the infant, to recreate the sensations, the discoveries, the emotional experiences and the gradual realization of identity as a baby first encounters the world.

15

Reaching out for the world

Anthony Storr

The birth of a wanted child is, in the ordinary family, attended with rejoicing. Even before the baby has arrived, both parents will have speculated endlessly about this new person, and once birth has taken place, and the sex of the child is known, the baby, automatically and inevitably, becomes the centre of a web of fantasy. What will he be like? Will he be dark or fair, intelligent or dull? Will he be like me, or like you, or like some remote ancestor? Perhaps he will be a creative genius, or will make his mark in some undreamed-of fashion. Whatever he may turn into, he is certainly unique. There has never before been anyone just like him, and there never will be again. For the moment, the hopes and fears of the parents focus on this tiny, new atom, who can carry so many speculations just because he is not yet a person with limits, but an undefined bundle of infinite possibilities.

Speculations about infants are not, of course, confined to parents. Since psychoanalysis began to emphasize the importance of the earliest years or even weeks of life for the future of the individual, there have been many attempts to reconstruct some picture of a baby's subjective experience. Direct observation of infants is gradually confirming a good deal of what used to be inspired guesswork. Our knowledge, however, is sadly incomplete, and it will never be possible to grasp the world of a baby in its entirety, because, quite simply, babies cannot talk. Nevertheless, unless we make some attempt to rediscover the buried imaginative experience which comprises so much of childhood, we shall never comprehend our own so-called adult emotions, nor be capable of giving our children the understanding and the love which should be their birthright.

The most essential feature of human infancy and childhood is the length of time during which the child is dependent, weak and helpless. Over a quarter of the total life-span of a human being is taken up with the journey from birth to physical maturity; whilst psychological maturity remains an ever-receding goal, attainable only in theory. It is this long period of dependence and weakness that contributes most to the child's picture of the world about him and of the adults who compose it: and it is the persistence of this childish world-view which, in later life, gives rise to the emotional problems and the difficulties between persons that are so characteristic a feature of the human condition. Throughout our lives, whatever our achievements, whatever love we may inspire, we still remain vulnerable: for none of us ever forgets what it was to be a helpless infant, totally at the mercy of persons and forces beyond our control.

It is only very gradually that a child becomes aware of its existence as a separate entity. The beginning of life must be passed in the kind of dream an adult may experience again during illness or whilst waking from an anaesthetic. Shadowy figures come and go; sensations, smells, comforts and discomforts intermittently interrupt the dream. There are shadows on the ceiling, unintelligible noises; hands lift, rearrange and settle. There is warmth and cold, hunger and satiety, wetness and dryness. Very early indeed there must be some perception of familiar landmarks; for babies removed from home will, on their return, show an anxious absorption in their environment instead of lying peacefully at rest.

Sometimes there is insecurity and fear. It is vital to be securely held and supported, and unskilful, uncertain handling provokes a violent protest. Noise is also alarming, especially when sudden; although the presence of a human face rapidly becomes a kind of talisman, so that sounds that frighten if no one is there do not do so if a face is visible. Indeed, the human face is one of the earliest features of the environment which a child distinguishes—although to a baby one face is at first much like another. A baby's needs can be fulfilled only by persons, but he cannot at first discriminate between them. A variable, but quite long, period of time passes before he can distinguish his mother as an individual from other people who may feed, cuddle or comfort him. By six months, however, he has accomplished this; and, although smell and other perceptions may play their part in recognition, it is by her face that a baby knows his mother, and it is her face to which he responds, by giving a smile that is no longer so easily elicited by other faces.

At the same time that he discovers other people, a baby begins to discover himself. Gradually he comes to define his own body: the arms and legs and hands that seem so far from the centre and yet are nevertheless attached to it: the big head, the thumb—the mouth that constitutes the core of comfort and the first and most vital means of contact with another person. Some time during the second half of the first year of life the world becomes divided into two: an 'I' and a 'not-I', each incompletely defined, each overlapping with the other, but nevertheless beginning to separate. To be conscious of where one's body begins and ends is such an achievement that, even years afterwards, in fever and in dream, the demarcation line between self and world can sometimes become blurred again. During illness, for example, many people can remember that they have experienced a kind of distortion of the image of their body, so that a thumb or the tongue seems disproportionately enormous. Often the perception of both time and space also becomes altered in illness, so that at such moments an adult may recapture what we imagine must be the infant's experience before order has been imposed upon the world, or time conceived as measurable duration.

How ignominious it is to be a child! To be so small that one can be picked up, to be moved around at the whim of others, fed or not fed, cleaned or left dirty, made happy or left to cry; it is surely so ultimate an indignity that it is not surprising that none of us ever recovers from it. For it is surely one of the basic fears of mankind that we shall be treated as *things* and not as *persons*: manipulated, pushed around by impersonal forces, treated as of no account by the powerful and superior. Each one of us is a tiny atom in an enormous universe; and, looked at objectively, none of us is likely to be of any ultimate importance in the scheme of things. But we cannot bear to be treated according to our deserts. We need the illusion that we count, that our individuality commands attention; and to be totally disregarded as a person is a kind of death in life against which we are compelled to fight with all our strength.

Halfway through the first year a baby becomes vulnerable as a person in a new way. He learns to fear the departure of the mother whom he has come to recognize, and so he clings

The beginning of life must be passed in a world of shadowy giants.

'How ignominious it is to be a child'—so small that your toy elephant is bigger than you.

to her and demands her presence even when his immediate physical needs are satisfied. He also becomes aware that there are people who are not his mother, strangers to whom he reacts with uncertainty and fear. No sooner are personal relations established than the severance of those relations becomes a threatening possibility. The infant becomes prey to those basic apprehensions that remain with us all our lives: the fear of being abandoned by those on whom we are dependent, and the fear of being harmed by those whom we do not know or trust.

To judge from adult experience, the ultimate horror is not to be ill-used, but to be treated as if we are of no account. A child who angers its parents at least has the power to move them; moreover, love and hate are so intimately connected that the existence of the one emotion automatically implies the possibility of its opposite. But we all remain vulnerable to the humiliation of being ignored. If, as children, we were actually disregarded or neglected we remain especially sensitive to slights, whether real or imagined. When Gulliver travelled to Brobdingnag he entered a world of huge creatures in whose hands he was powerless, but it is humiliation rather than weakness which really disturbs him:

That which gave me most Uneasiness among those Maids of Honour, when my Nurse carried me to visit them, was to see them use me without any Manner of Ceremony, like a Creature who had no Sort of Consequence.

Those shadowy giants who pass in and out of the child's world have it in their power to reinforce or to undermine his sense of his own existence as a person. The realization of his own identity, in fact, is only gradually built up through continued interaction with other people. The seriously neglected child may turn into an adult who fears his own disintegration: the loss of that sense of being 'I' which binds the disparate elements of personality into a seeming whole. People of this kind, like Humpty Dumpty, sit precariously upon a wall, forever in danger of being shattered into fragments.

There seems little doubt that, at first, the sense of being a continuing person depends upon continuity of care. If, for too long, no one is there, the void opens, we are cut off, we exist no longer. Volunteers who take part in experiments in personal isolation often demand to be released prematurely because, after a short period alone, they cannot believe that they have not been totally forgotten by the scientists conducting the experiment. A basic trust in the continuity of other people's concern and regard for us is as essential as the belief that the sun will rise, that spring will come again. Writers of science fiction have sometimes explored the horrors of discontinuity. The possibility, for instance, that a man could be deceived into thinking he was on earth whilst actually in a space-ship circling in the void—is an imaginative illustration of how a jolt can be given to reality capable of undermining an individual's sense of continuity both in himself and in his surroundings. In some forms of mental illness, a patient may believe that everyone else has changed: that friends he once knew and trusted are only actors playing parts. The discovery that things or people are not what they had seemed strikes at our own sense of our identity. The stability of personal identity is dependent upon the stability of our relatedness to an environment which, although it may and does change, does not suddenly alter its face completely in some totally unpredictable way.

The world in which small children dwell must seem to them both incomprehensible and capricious, in much the same way as the adult world appears to the hero of a novel by Kafka. The conduct of the giants may be regulated by some rule or other, but there is no way of discerning what this may be. The only guide a small child can possibly have is the state of his own feelings; and if what his parents do does not closely conform to what the child needs at the time, he is bound to feel sometimes that the world is an alarming place in which anything can happen, and in which he is totally at the mercy of arbitrary forces. An actual, recurrent failure on the part of parents to meet a child's needs, whether physical or emotional, may lead to so severe a fear of betrayal that trust is permanently impaired. Starvation, whether it be of attention, food, or affection may so deprive a child that it grows into an adult who cannot risk loving, because showing love to another makes him vulnerable to feelings of rejection and fears of attack. Such persons withdraw into an island of schizoid isolation, where they are protected from danger but have become inaccessible to love which they dare neither to give nor to receive.

To such a child, it is the *power* of adults which both terrifies and excites envy. As he grows up, it is the problem of making himself felt which will chiefly preoccupy him, rather than that of making himself agreeable. It may happen that the whole object of his life becomes that of insuring that he is invulnerable—in a position so powerful that he cannot easily be attacked and from which he can exercise domination. He retreats to an ivory tower in which he will suffer the pangs of isolation, but which at any rate serves to protect him from involvement and therefore from pain.

We can all detect in ourselves remnants of this particular child's-eye view, but those who have never learned to see beyond this suffer a sad fate. There is little point in a life which is lived in an emotional vacuum, and even the greatest achievement or the most powerful position will not protect a man against the sense of futility inevitably afflicting those condemned to emotional isolation.

Fortunately, most babies and small children receive sufficient continuity of care to give them a basic trust in the giant figures who tend them; and, at the same time, are able to develop an increasingly solid sense of identity. The existence of trust, however, itself raises new problems, precisely because it makes possible new kinds of relationships. The child moves on from being dependent on adults for its existence, to being dependent upon them for love. If we are to reach our full potentiality it is not enough that we should be acknowledged and taken into account. We need also to be approved of and affectionately cherished. To become susceptible to love is to become vulnerable to anger and disapproval. One cannot be capable of joy without being capable of sadness; and so it follows that a child who becomes capable of being a fully integrated happy human being is also a child capable of experiencing depression.

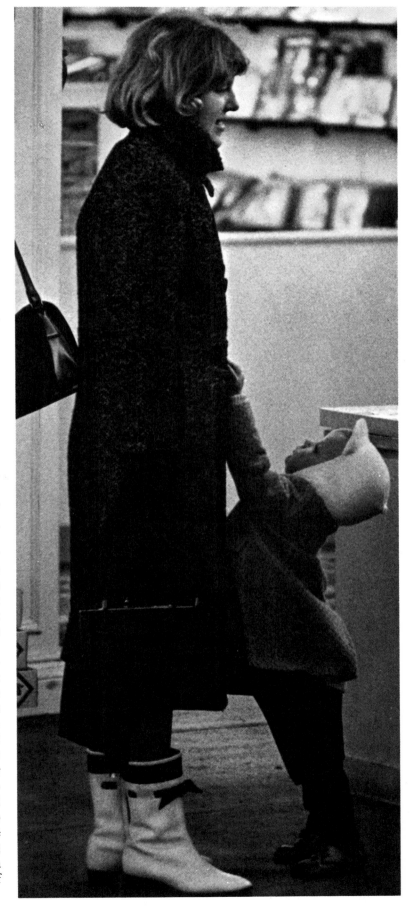

A new sort of dependence is now established. Continuity of existence may be ensured; continuing happiness remains precarious. The giants are always there, but they are not always the same. Sometimes they are kind and gentle, caressing, comforting, smiling. At other times they show a different face: disapproving, punishing, angry. It is hard to know which face will be presented; but gradually the child learns to accommodate itself to what must originally seem arbitrary; to discover what pleases and what displeases.

In this way a new dichotomy is created. The world, already divided into self and not-self, becomes yet further split into *good* and *evil*. It is very early that the child eats the fruit of this particular tree, and finds out that love is conditional on *good* behaviour. The images formed of parental figures at this stage persist through life. The Virgin Mary and the witch may seem unrelated; but they are opposite aspects of the same coin. For if a mother can be good, protective and loving, it follows automatically that she can also be bad, destructive and hating. C. G. Jung describes one aspect of this double image in his autobiography:

My mother was a very good mother to me. She had a hearty animal warmth, cooked wonderfully, and was most companionable and pleasant. . . . She held all the conventional opinions a person was obliged to have, but then her unconscious personality would suddenly put in an appearance. . . . There was an enormous difference between my mother's two personalities. That was why as a child I often had anxiety dreams about her. By day she was a loving mother, but at night she seemed uncanny. Then she was like one of those seers who is at the same time a strange animal, like a priestess in a bear's cave.

If we need the love of another we are at the mercy of that love being withdrawn or turned into hate; and those who have the most power to reassure us are the very persons who are most easily able to frighten and cruelly undermine our confidence.

In myth and fairy story these opposite aspects of parental figures are personified: the wholly evil versus the wholly good. The child lives in a black and white world; and it is a world which, as adults, we all enjoy re-entering. It is a great though dangerous relief to shed our sophisticated grasp of the complexities of personality and to pretend once more that the enemy is entirely evil and the hero entirely good. This is one reason why we enjoy detective stories and Westerns—or at least used to do so before they both became 'psychological'. The child's world is one of simple, powerful hates and loves because it is based on subjective needs: that is, upon how people appear in the light of what the child wants, or fears, or fails to obtain, not upon how people actually are in reality.

Thus, when Red Riding Hood finds the wolf in her grandmother's place she might be symbolically making the discovery that grandmothers do not always display the same face: that, for example, grandmotherly kindness and solicitude can easily turn into overprotectiveness and a destructive possessiveness. But she is unable to relate the two figures. The wolf and the grandmother remain separate, and the idea that good and bad can be fused within the same person, or comprise parts of a single relationship, is a conception which some human beings never succeed in grasping. The time at which a baby first recognizes his mother as *one* person with these different facets varies. If development proceeds normally, this stage is probably reached somewhere between the sixth and twelfth month, but the possibility of regression to a state in which her image is divided into two again remains latent within us all. Images of the good and evil mother are universal, since every child may be supposed to experience both love and protection on the one hand, and frustration and deprivation on the other. The ease with which even supposedly adult persons can attach such images to actual people and thus slip back into the world of childhood is sometimes horrifying. Thousands of innocent, harmless old women have been tortured and burned to death because men have attributed to them the power to harm and to destroy which the small child believes to be the prerogative of the mother in her evil aspect. A mother who is always punishing or rejecting may indeed be a kind of witch who does permanent emotional damage to her children. Although most mothers are not like this most of the time, they are bound to be so occasionally, and so the image of the witch has a universal appeal, and she easily becomes a scapegoat who can be held responsible for the immaturities, the failures and the persistent childishness which are part of all of us. To read *Malleus Maleficarum*, that fifteenth century Inquisitors' manual, is to enter a mythological world in which the power of witchcraft is believed to cause disease, infatuation, impotence and every emotional problem for which a modern patient might consult a psychiatrist. If we blame the witch we need not face our own guilts and our own failure to escape the toils of childhood. Let us torture her and burn her, therefore, for she relieves us of the burden of our humanity.

The example of the witch is but one instance of how an image, conceived in infancy, can exert a continuing influence. There are many others. Because of our weakness and helplessness in early childhood, even positive images of parental figures are bound to be distorted. Impressionable as we are, we tend to believe that parents are so strong, so clever or so wise that we can never hope to emulate them; and so we fail to make full use of whatever gifts we possess because we think that we can never match ourselves with such august prototypes. It is clearly a consequence of this that the conventional image of a great national leader is often so idealized as to bear little relation to reality. Ambitious men driven by the desire for power are seldom agreeable or generous; but the masses will not hear a word of criticism against a leader whom they admire and upon whom they depend; and so the errors of judgment, impatience, intolerance and ruthlessness which are characteristic of 'the great' are forgotten pieces of driftwood upon the sea of adulation that washes around the hero.

The world of the small child is, we conclude, peopled by mythological figures who bear little resemblance to real persons, but who are personifications of the child's own projected needs and fears. The child both requires protection and also wants to break free of it, so that the loving arms which enfold him are at one time a longed-for refuge, at another a confining prison. Freud, over sixty years ago, shattered the conventional picture of childhood innocence and showed us that infantile loves and jealousies can be as intense as the adult passions of which they are the precursors. Freud's successors have demonstrated that the infant's world is not only sensual, but also shot through with aggression. The reason for this is not merely that parental figures are frustrating or angry,

although on occasion, they are bound to be so: it is also a reflection of the child's urgent drive towards self-assertion and independence. It is not surprising that myth and fairy-story contain so much violence, nor that they evoke such deep echoes within us all. The hero myths with which we are regaled as soon as we are capable of grasping a story appeal to us so powerfully because they portray an inner world of which we all have had experience. These tales are violent tales because the process of emerging from childhood is a tough and often painful struggle which demands courage, endurance and strength. The typical pattern is that the youngest, most disregarded son sets forth upon a dangerous exploit. Not until he has overcome all kinds of obstacles, fought dragons and killed monsters, can he win freedom and love. In order to win Andromeda, Perseus has to kill first the Gorgon Medusa and then a sea-monster; nor can he ascend the throne until he has also disposed of Acrisius, his maternal grandfather. Such violent action may seem remote from the decorous passivity which Western adults tend to expect of their children; but it is characteristic of the fantasy life of childhood. For such myths are concerned with a psychological reality. Every child is threatened by dangers, since he is a small uncertain atom in an immense world with which he is not at first equipped to deal. He is also surrounded by monstrously powerful adults who may and should protect, but who also have to be overcome if he is ever to be independent. The most helpful mother can be a witch; the most powerfully protective father a tyrant; and this is true of the best parents as it is of the worst.

In a happy home where a child is welcomed and cherished, the protective, loving support of the parents instils sufficient basic confidence for a gradually increasing mastery of the external world to be attained. The more a child feels himself loved, the more he is able to do without parental protection and overcome the tendency to cling closely to mother's apron-strings, which prevents him from exploring his surroundings independently. Only when a child carries within him the strength which comes from having experienced love can he risk facing more and more of the world alone. As he slowly emerges from the mist of infancy his perception of external reality becomes less clouded by subjective distortion, and his sense of his own identity and of his own actual capabilities is slowly confirmed by experience. However mature he eventually becomes—and human beings vary vastly in the degree of maturity they attain—he will never wholly escape from that cloudy confusion in which he entered the world. The images formed in his infant mind will continue to haunt him in dream and fantasy, and influence every relationship he makes.

A child's development can be seen as an uphill journey towards a meeting with the giant parental figures descending from Olympus. Often the two never meet, and the ostensible adult remains a child at heart, always looking to others to tell him how to live. But, as the child grows larger, the giants seem smaller, and if the two are able finally to confront each other they will see that each is the same as the other. The child within the adult recognizes the adult within the child: a human being, no more, no less; with equal capacity for cruelty and for compassion, for suffering and for joy.

Much has been written about babies,
in this book and elsewhere, by people
who profess to know about them.
One of the most satisfactory recorded
comments, however, came not from
a psychiatrist or a pediatrician, or
even from a fond mother, but
from the American statesman
Benjamin Franklin.
As his country's minister to France,
Franklin witnessed, in August 1783,
the first flight of the Montgolfier
brothers' hot air balloon. A sceptic
in the crowd asked, 'But what is the
use of these balloons?' 'But what
use,' Franklin replied, 'is a new
born baby?'

The day of birth

No one is quite sure just what effect a mother has on her baby before it is born. But the baby itself, in the forty weeks from its conception to its birth, goes through an incredible growth—proportionately more than it will do during its whole future lifetime—from a microscopic organism to a living creature. In the darkness of the womb its eyes have begun to move, its eyelids have winked, its fingers have flexed, its brain has begun to develop. Birth will be life's greatest challenge to its nervous system.

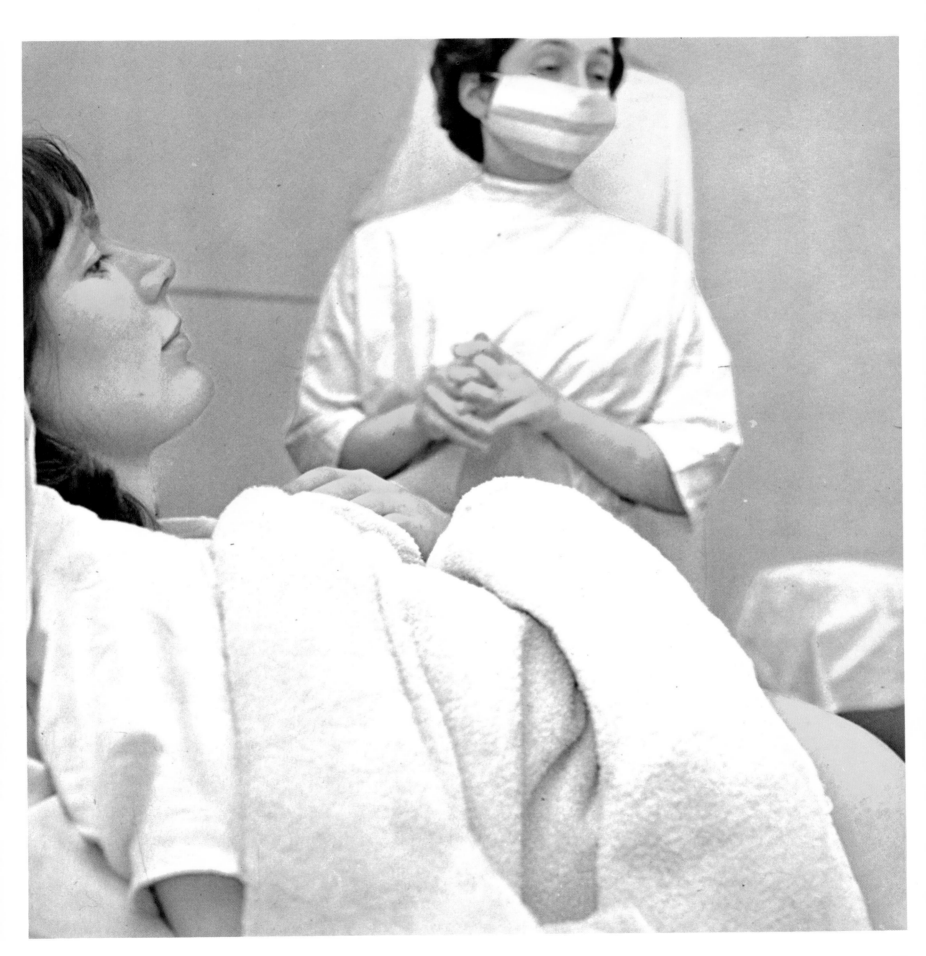

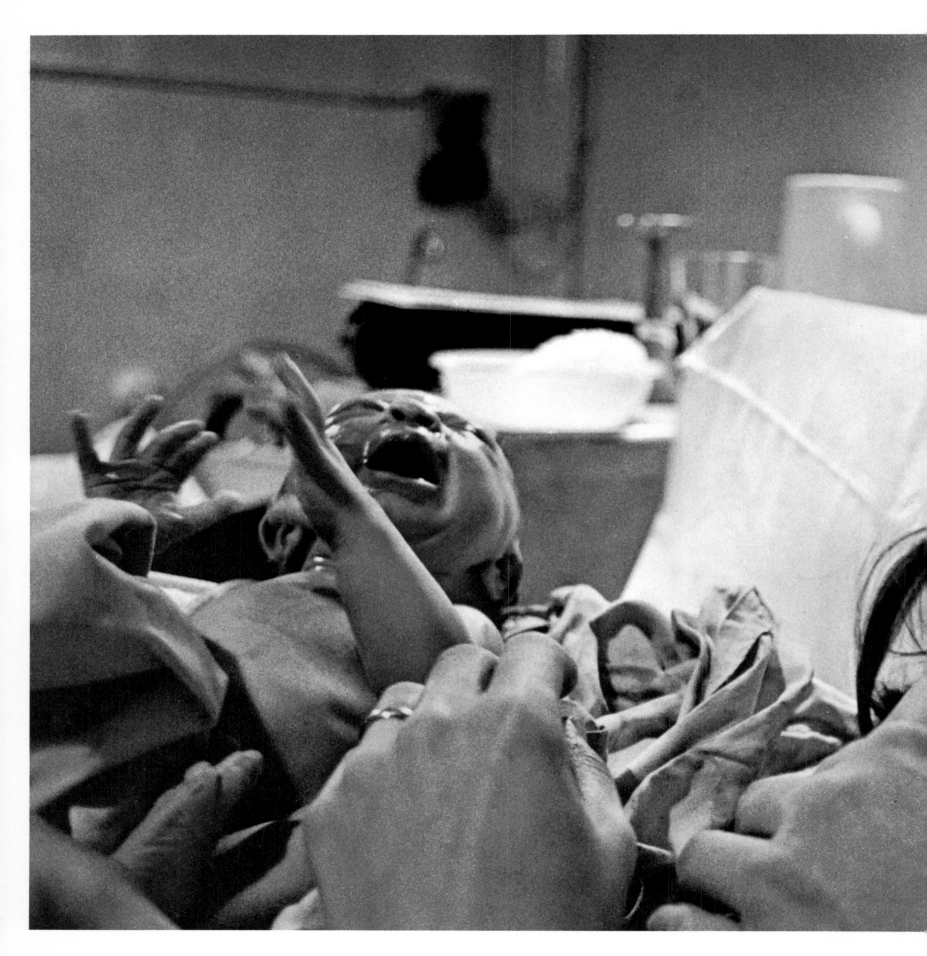

Four babies are born every second,
125 million a year. Each one is
unique.

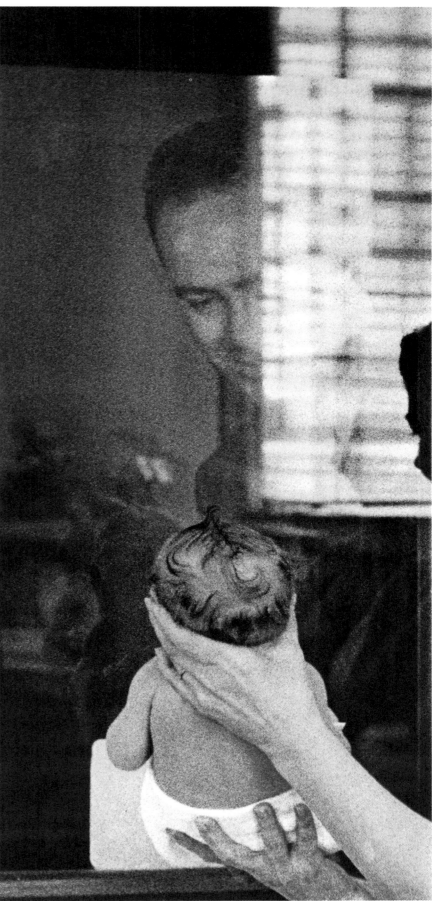

The hand cannot be the tool of the will until brain and eye are co-ordinated. Eyes begin to focus at eight weeks. But it is only at seven months that a baby can consciously see, reach out and grasp its father's hand.

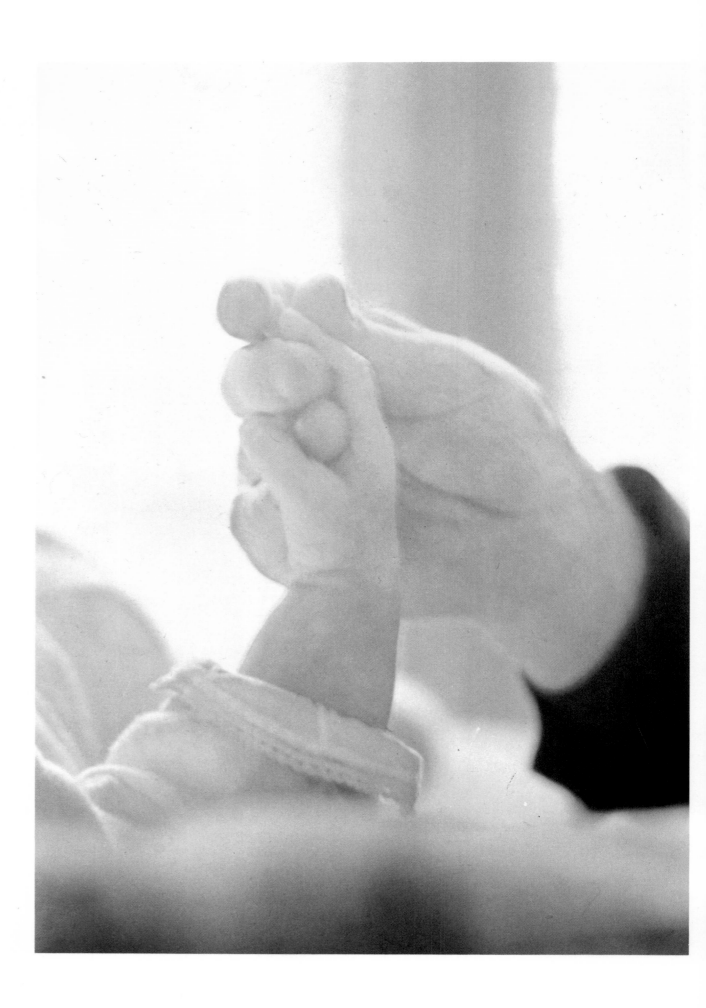

When a baby cries and is fed it is not only nourished but enjoys a feeling of safety, contentment and probably power.

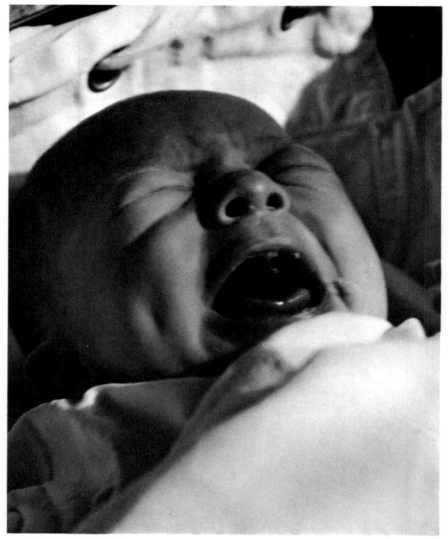

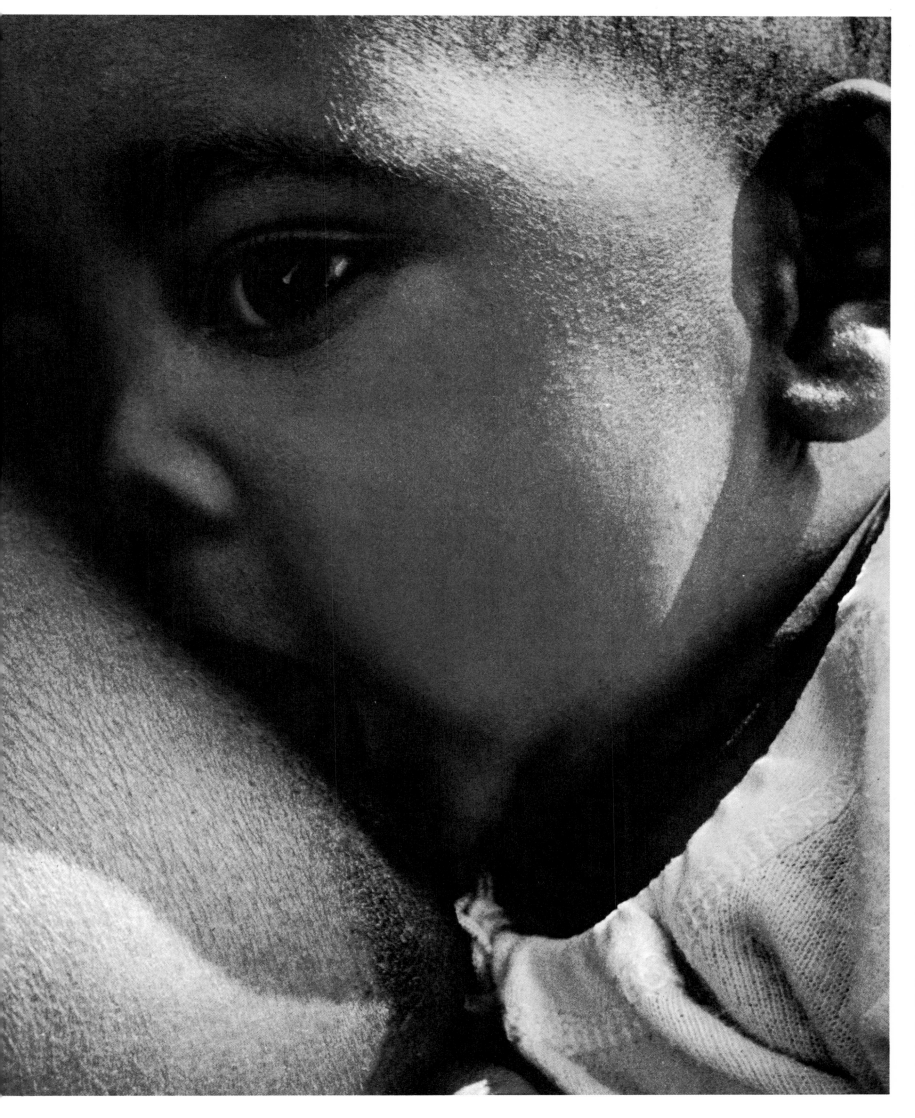

Even when they can really see, babies still have only the vaguest idea of such things as where they end and where their cots begin. Paradoxically, they learn the dividing line between self and non-self only by exploring their own bodies. At twenty-five weeks babies can begin to touch their toes.

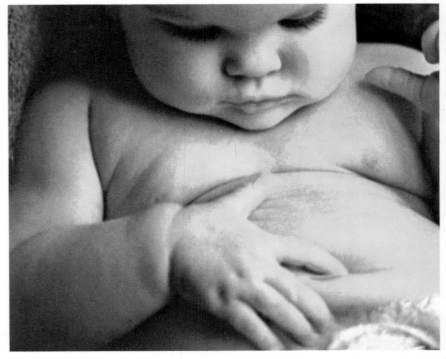

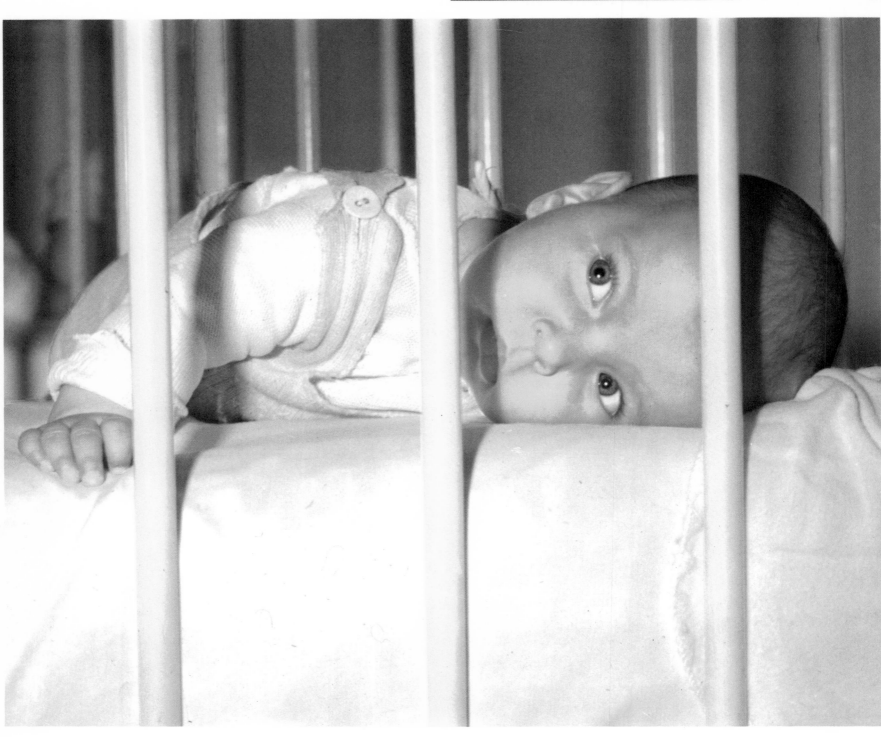

But whatever their physical
limitations, they are not at all limited
in the delight they have and give.
And after about the twentieth week
babies begin to laugh.

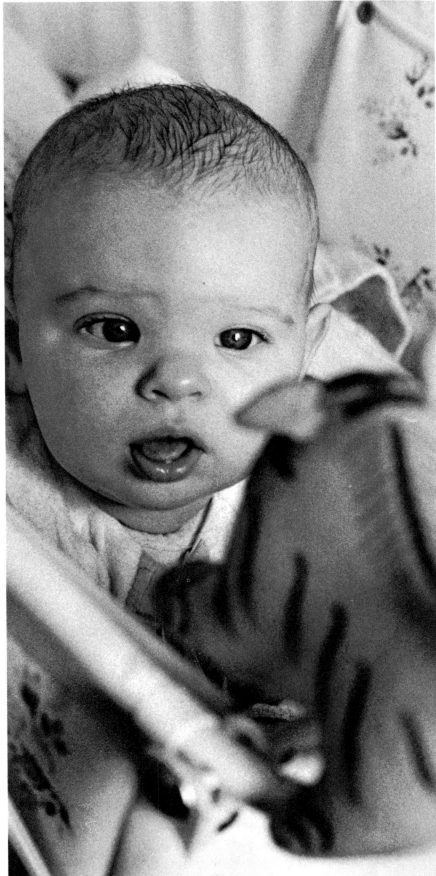

Smiling often occurs in the first weeks.

Experts are not sure why. Some are even convinced that a smile does not start as a sign of joy but is merely one of several neutral physical responses. Parents, the theory runs, like smiles and encourage them until, at the end of a year, smiling has become permanently associated with pleasure. In short, babies theoretically could just as easily learn to frown their delight.

Mothers, who ought to know, are not much impressed by theories.

The African child (right), his ears already pierced according to tribal custom, is likely to live in temperatures up to 117° F., and will probably not be weaned before his fourth year. The Eskimo boy (left) is already eating solid food in his first few weeks and must be protected against temperatures as low as minus 74° F. What they and most babies born in primitive societies have in common is a view of the world into which a mother's head and shoulder securely protrude.

'I could not point to any need in childhood so strong as that for a father's protection'
—Sigmund Freud

Philippino father carrying his baby in a shawl.

London father helping his baby learn to walk.

A father's hand is like a shield

Yoruba tribesman in Western Nigeria holds his son in a carrying cloth.

American father burps his baby.

Erigpactsá Indian father bathes his son in a Brazilian river.

You *are* your brother's keeper

Despite the lamentable fact that brothers and sisters nowadays are often called siblings, they are still indispensable to growing up. Your big brother may belt you, but he knows things like how to make slingshots, and play marbles. Your sister is only a girl but she has a way with wayward shoelaces. Next to parents, in fact, brothers and sisters are a most notable example of something that is hard to live with, but impossible to live without.

A tearful Lapp boy in traditional costume, except for tennis shoes, makes a strong play for sisterly help in tying his shoelace.

44

A watchful young member of the Australian Pitjantjatjara tribe learns from his big brother how to conduct a raid on a spinifex plant. The catch —snakes, rats, and perhaps a bandicoot or two—will be baked under a layer of earth, and served for lunch. In the tribe the skills of hunting, complicated rituals and customs, tribal songs and legends are taught to the young by their elders when the children are only three to four years old, an age when civilized children seem hardly able to learn their ABCs.

The burden of a family

It is supposed to afflict and affect parents only. But children, early on, are initiated, too.

This Indian boy carrying his baby sister to the steps of a seventeenth-century church in Chichicastenango, Guatemala, has a sense of responsibility that is almost parental.

Above: Two London babies get used to the idea of having to share sleeping quarters.

Below: Two American brothers react in different ways to the problem of getting milk into their newest relative.

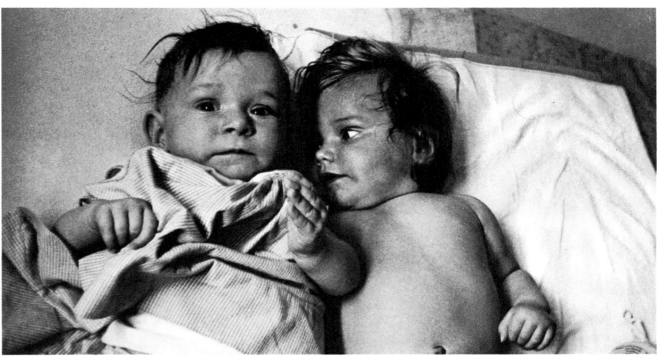

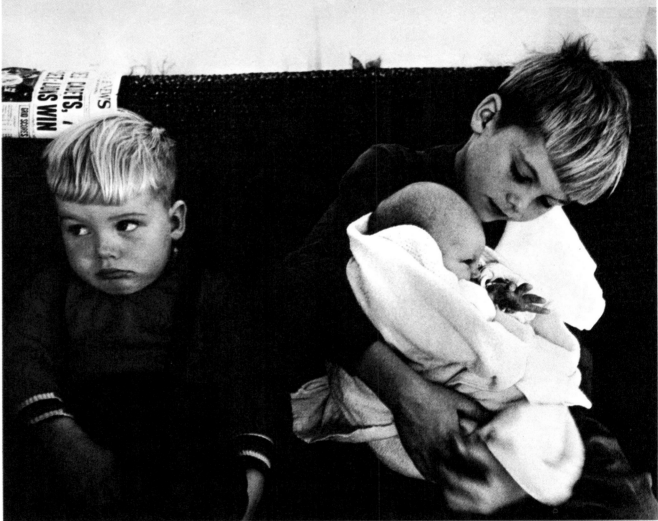

Communion with the world outside

England: Clumsy but earnest attempt
to test, with buttercup, who likes
butter best.

Sardinia: Animated group discussion,
the way they've seen their parents
do it.

First lessons in relativity

The emotional lessons in interdependence learned in a family tend to be the same everywhere. Youth learns from age, rebels against custom, and eventually inherits responsibility. But the ground rules are very different in different parts of the world.

These Canadian Eskimo children, securely surrounded by mothers and aunts, lead a semi-nomadic existence which is the life of their family and their people. Times are changing

however. Under new settlement schemes, their children may come to live in one place and learn, from schools, how to breed reindeer rather than hunt them.

50

A Bedouin Arab family of the Duru tribe. These children together with their parents and their family possessions—two goats and a camel—spend all their lives wandering the desert and looking for scarce grazing lands. From puberty, the daughter will henceforth be masked and veiled like her mother. The son will one day inherit the dagger, an heirloom, that hangs at his father's belt.

51

Gunning for play, fiddling for real

Family outings can be just for fun or strictly necessary. In either case they impose a role to be played. In Rochester, N.Y. (below) boys and girls ride tin tanks at a fun fair. On a street corner in Katmandu, a section of Nepal children of the same age join a family band playing for money.

They belong to a gypsy-like group called the Gaine, Hindus who live high in the mountains. Their skill with the sarangi, a kind of fiddle, is handed down from father to son, as are their great store of traditional songs.

A growing independence

The journey from helpless beginnings
to the beginnings of independence
must pass through a period of
savouring all the things of the world
all by yourself. Curiosity killed a cat
but how can you keep from
wondering what makes the water
come out?

Backyard water pump, U.S.A.

Sheer exhultation, Fire Island, New York.

Getting a drink the hard way, Johannesburg, South Africa.

And miles to go before she sleeps . . .

The garden is white and wonderful, deep in an English winter. The girl is quite capable all by herself of rescuing a white rabbit from the snow. Anyone who doubts that this is a major step towards independence and maturity should try abducting an outsized rabbit who doesn't much want to be taken home.

Learning

This five-year-old English girl is learning how to count with an abacus—a counting machine probably first devised in China some six hundred years before Christ. That she is doing so at all is not so much a sign of creeping antiquarianism in her school, as a symptom of one of the principle preoccupations of our age. Today more children are going to school than ever could have been imagined. Trying to learn about learning is a pressing international concern. Meanwhile with the supply of teachers dwindling proportionately, all sorts of teaching devices are being pressed into service—brand new programmed teaching machines, closed-circuit television, old fashioned counting rods and even the abacus. Today's children are the occasionally bewildered beneficiaries.

Ever since a gifted young German named Friedrich Froebel first invented the kindergarten in 1837 and began trying to make learning a form of child's play, professional educators have been formally pointing out what good teachers have always informally understood: that children are curious animals whose learning process moves, often in fits and starts, by strange and diverse ways. This is one of the points made by Edward Blishen, the author of the essay which begins on the next page. A successful university lecturer, author of textbooks and children's books (including a best-seller about English secondary school life called *The Roaring Boys*)—the author examines the 'rich confusion of being a child'. In this day and age, he feels that just learning to be a tolerable human being is fantastically difficult.

Children, learning in many ways in many parts of the world, alone and in small groups, as well as in formal classrooms, are the subject of the accompanying picture essay.

The dialogue between teacher and taught

Edward Blishen

With the very young, anywhere—provided they are healthy and reasonably free and happy—it's simple. Learning is living: and the other way round. This is a matter of observation, with which the theorists have long agreed. I've had the experience familiar to all who've taught older children in a conventional school, and at the same time have had small children of their own: the experience of moving from the professional struggle to get learning going, to the parental struggle to keep learning within the bounds of adult energy and patience.

As soon as speech makes it possible comes the torrent of questions. 'How many toys in my toy-box?' His mother, for whom this is one question too many on a long morning, says: 'Oh, a great many.' He frowns. 'Why don't you tell me how many?' Then he darkly rephrases this: '*Why don't you know?*' His last word is meant to hurt even more deeply: 'I shall ask Daddy when he comes in.' Daddy, meanwhile, may be trying at school to stir up in his older children some interest in, say, elementary algebra. Much of that intense spontaneous curiosity, that once made them mother-botherers, has gone. It's true that for his older children the relevance of algebra to the lives they are leading (or are likely to lead) seems small. They happen not to be the sort of lives that will be made perceptibly worse by ignorance of algebra. This matter of relevance is very important, as we shall see.

For the very young, too, there is the earliest attempt to read: practised on the labels on bottles on the breakfast table. 'Up and down and up—that's N. . . . Two strokes and one across—that's H.' There's the continual attempt to tidy up the world of everyday objects by applying to those objects such notions of logic and science as the child has acquired: 'If it's a brown haystack, it will be brown bread. If it's a white haystack, it will be white bread.' Or the child may experimentally bring to bear on an object not only his early feeling for scientific law, but also his sentimental experience, which suggests that nothing whatever is beyond the reach of sympathy: of a new moon, 'Poor broken moon!'

Then, still at this early stage, there's the endless inquiry into the limits of things: as we climb to the top deck of a bus, 'Can we see the whole world?' There's the discovery of the incantation as a weapon against fear—the small muttered assertion that is intended to keep danger at bay. One of my sons quite saw that Santa Claus was a friendly and generous figure—yet he had that horrifying mass of beard, and he came down the chimney when you were asleep. So my son's incantation, which he was to be heard murmuring at intervals during the year, ran: 'Don't hurt you, Father Christmas!' It was part of a small set speech he had built up on this principle, covering his fear of being knocked down by a bus—'Don't hurt you, bus!'—and ending with a phrase intended to ward off the menace of our noisy local yearly carnival: 'Don't hurt you, Barnet Fair!' There's also the heaping up of conquered words: 'What's boasting?' And, often enough, the unexpected reception of a definition: 'Well then, I *like* boasting.'

The drive here is obvious. The world must be mastered, well enough at any rate for the child to be able to make his way through it as a reasonably competent human being: and there is a great deal to be known, and a great balance to be sought. The balance is between the inward person and the world outside him: between the vast and often awful possibilities of the imagination and the reality which is bearable simply because it is real.

The adult represents a promise that this balance can be achieved. The trouble with the adult, and especially with the adult as a teacher, is that he may have lost all touch with the rich confusion of being a child. His teaching may be drearily formal, or may miss the point, or may simply come at the wrong time. 'Well, thunder,' he says, 'thunder is caused by lightning. Lightning is very hot, and it makes the air expand —that means the air swells up and gets bigger, and so . . .' But this has become a procession of unfamiliar words and unimaginable ideas: the child resorts for relief to fantasy spiced with verbal horseplay. 'The clouds go bang. They hit each other and go *bang bang bang*. Someone pushes them and they go *bang bang bang bang bang*.' The adult turns pale and tells the child not to be silly. But the silliness is a very reasonable gesture of resistance: what can't be understood must be beaten down with noise and fooling.

Again, the adult may not grasp how much in this early learning may be a desire for mastery of some small set form— the story or explanation often repeated and always exactly in the same words. Opposition to the variant can be intense. One night, for fun, you mis-recite the last line of the nursery rhyme: 'She shall have cobwebs on the end of her nose,' you say. And at once you are at the centre of a punishing whirlwind of fists and feet. '*No no no no!*' He is very angry. This had been a small mastery, the little security of something learned, and you have shaken it.

But though teaching and learning, here as at other points in life, often fail to mesh with one another, learning does triumphantly go on. Much of it—and for this the human race must be grateful—does not depend on the adult being resourceful or having deep insight. The interplay of a child with his environment is full of accidents of learning. And adults sometimes teach best when they are unaware of doing so: when they are being themselves, doing or saying what can be experimentally copied.

Most children, fairly early, love simply to be spectators of the adult world in action. Among their earliest classrooms may be the family party, when they sit listening to the marvellous conversation of adults: much of it inexplicable, but all of it to be plundered for ideas, phrases, shreds of information, revelations of the way things go. I used to pray, when I was small and out for a walk with my father, that we should meet another adult, so that I could listen to their strange, miraculous speech: every subject they touched on had magnificence. They exchanged banalities about the weather and I trembled with satisfaction. . . . Again, there's unscheduled learning of this kind whenever children watch their elders carrying out any activity whatever: paying fares on a bus, packing a suitcase, mending or making. In this marvellous wide sense, living is learning: and a child's instinct that this is so may lie partly behind his impatience whenever his elders opt out of life, lying down on beaches, snoozing on Sunday afternoons. One of the great gulfs between the young and the adult is that the young see no point in not getting on with life.

Eight-year-olds at a London school learn about fractions by tracing different sized segments of a circle.

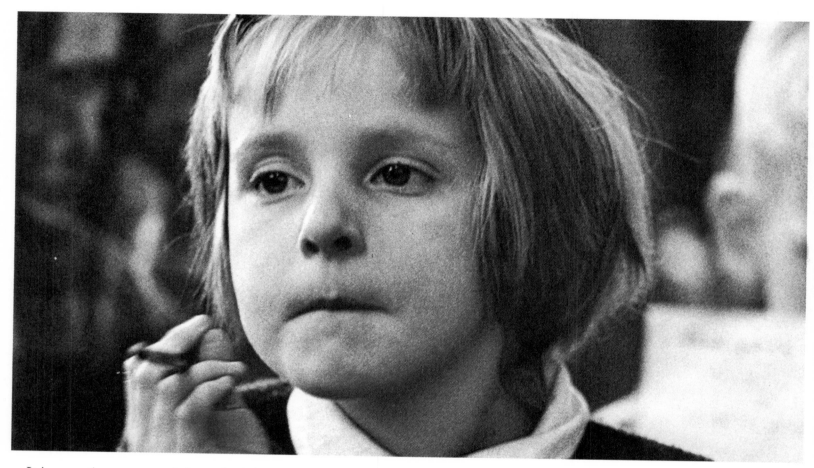

It is sometimes assumed that scheduled learning—even the earliest examples of it—is of a different order from this: that it introduces quite new notions of discipline and compulsion: that as often as not it involves struggle. Well, certainly struggle is often present; but this commonly arises from a defect in the teaching, or from something awry in the circumstances, rather than from a failure of resolution or goodwill on the part of the learner. (Failure of energy there may sometimes be: I think we should remind ourselves more often than we do what a fantastically difficult and exacting thing it is to embrace all the learning involved in becoming a tolerable human being.) No child wants to wet his bed, once he has had the experience of the choice between comfort and discomfort. To be able to dress oneself is a superb act of mastery and mark of independence, against which nothing is to be said. No child wants *not* to learn, provided he is reasonably happy and the learning is timely and suitable. Failures, together with lapses and back-slidings, may arise because an adult has been clumsy, or has overlooked a difficulty: or simply because there is, to the side of the thing learned, a piece of unlearned life. A grasp of time, for example, comes late in the day: a child who seems for the moment to have unlearned something may simply have forgotten that it was time to do it.

As to discipline and compulsion: they are deeply written into any learning whatever, be it accidental or contrived. Children, one knows, have a punctiliousness of their own, which is sometimes more exacting than that of adults. I once taught six-year-olds in the junior department of a preparatory school, crossing for one lesson a week from the senior depart-

ment several hundred yards away. (I had first, I must say—before I could teach them at all—to discover again what it was to be six years old. I had addressed them, in my earliest lessons, as though they were shrunken savants, suffering from slight handicaps in the matter of vocabulary.) My class would never wait for me in their room, but would collect at the main door of the school, eager to hurry me into my desk. They would surround me, seize my arms, bear me upstairs. 'You're late,' they would cry, though I never really was: 'You're late, and we shall miss a bit of our story.' They were tetchier than the tetchiest adult. I was, from their point of view, a very poorly disciplined teacher.

And so, indeed, to school: at any rate, in those parts of the world that have as yet the sometimes shaky blessing of schooling. I say 'shaky' because I believe we have a long way to go before we shall have learned to match in the forms of our teaching the marvellous teachability of the young. Let us look at what is still common experience: at the sheer abruptness with which school begins, and the degree of the unfamiliar and forbidding with which we often stamp the earliest moments of schooling. You are five years old, perhaps, and it is the most enormous building you have ever known. Indeed, until now you have known no building larger than a house. Some houses have alarmed you, with their habit of having more rooms than you can account for; but on the whole, houses have been manageable. The strangest door in a house *probably* led to a bedroom, or a bathroom: and these are rooms you understand. But this is a building beyond your grasp; and it is filled with strangers, who are using it for inscrutable purposes. You have never at once met so many strangers and so many purposes beyond your experience. It's a place, moreover, from which familiar characters, from Mother downwards, are specifically excluded. You have never before known a building which was not in some way for the use of mothers and other friendly people.

And suddenly *time* is important. Except vaguely, in terms of bedtime and teatime, you have never before come under the rule of the clock. You have never made an appointment with the various parts of the day. Time has been a wash of light coming and going: its divisions have been gentle and not peremptory. Now the day is ruled by bells, and by concepts of being on time and being late. Life has suddenly become a threatening bully.

The bully strikes at all your habits. It is no longer possible, for example, to speak as you had been accustomed to speak— as the need welled up in you. And it's more than speech that the bully prohibits . . . noises, sudden hurrahs and hosannas, the groans, the loud soliloquies: all the habits of utterance and noise are brought to an end. If there is something to be said, you must put up your hand and wait to be permitted to say it; and it must conform to some curious idea of what it is *sensible* to say. You are presented at once with the problem of what is sensible and what is not.

Many of the world's schools, as places, try hard to soften this suddenness, to keep the bully at bay. But too often, how much too small is the attempt they make to ease children gently from the world of home, and spontaneous learning, to this other world of school, and learning directed and deliberate. It is not wholly a matter of gentleness—though it is terribly easy for the adult, through failure of imagination, to be ungentle to children. It is also that here, in this transition, lies the whole future of a child's attitude to learning. He will not—and no one, however intellectually energetic and curious, ever could—retain the whole of his present appetite for knowledge and skill. Part of the drive that makes him potentially such an eager learner will fade as he achieves a normal mastery of life. His curiosity will shrink defeated— simply because he is a limited human being—from a vast range of phenomena. But there is within him now a quality of concern with the world and with ideas about the world— there is this superb spontaneous identification of living with learning—that ought in its essence to remain within him throughout his schooling, and beyond that throughout his whole adult life.

Whether it will do so depends on his attitude to schooling: for, willy-nilly, it is in school that much of his learning will now go on. So school, early school, should be at great pains to avoid seeming, suddenly, an inimical way of life: an institution that kidnaps a child from his world of childhood, and imprisons him in too much unfamiliar formality.

The work of the great educationists of the last century has brought about a humanization of many of our primary schools, *as places*. Fewer of them, *as places*, resemble the first school I went to myself, forty years ago: which was truly large, a warren of severe classrooms, whose geography I never did grasp, where we sat in stiff desks, two to a desk, in a general environment as of some small court room, forty minute

human beings in the dock. Our teacher was a stout comfortable lady—named Miss Stout, as it happened; and when we ached with solid sitting, she would let us get up, one by one, and draw in chalk on the blackboards that ran round the walls of the room. I remember *my* drawing, which I repeated daily while I was in that class: it was of a wheatsheaf—half a dozen curving lines this way, half a dozen curving lines that way, and a line round the middle to hold the sheaf together. It was not much, but it was something.

Our dynamos—for we were full of curiosity dashed, energy and speech inhibited—hummed and spat in that unsuitable setting. Of being alarmed by it all I remember much—of learning I remember little beyond discovering how to read silently: it happened one afternoon, I was reading some slight story about a hen in a farmyard, and I was half-tempted to shriek when I found the words reading themselves *inside* me —they seemed to tickle, as if I'd swallowed feathers. But I didn't shriek. Shrieking was not thought to be part of learning, in those days.

But though there are now rather fewer primary school classrooms in the world as rigid and dingy as that, and fewer school buildings as hostile to the child, there nevertheless are many that are unsuitable, architecturally and in their failure to be sensitive to the extraordinary natural eagerness of the young. We are still far, almost everywhere, from making of our schools places where the true teachability of our children can be seized and sustained.

To see why this is so we must look again at the nature of children and the real nature, at this point in human development, of learning.

First, small children are noisy: they are appallingly noisy, and it is important that they should be so. For self-discipline, of the order that makes the adult for much of the time silent, does not belong to this period of life, and ought not to belong to it. The noise that young children make is knit up with their manner of learning. They need at times to talk to themselves, to shout at themselves, to assume voices and utter strange dialogues, as though they were several persons at once. Often they work out ideas in this way. I remember my own children:

'He was a baddie.'
'He wasn't, he was a goodie.'
'Was.'
'Wasn't.'
'He wasn't a goodie—he was horrible.'
'He was a *horrible goodie*.'
'Goodies aren't ever horrible.'

And so on. It wasn't nonsense: it was a vital form of learning. Silent thought is, after all, a late achievement. So children need to think aloud at times: they also often need to think aloud together.

In a really free classroom, small children talk to one another endlessly: and though much of the talk is fantasy (fantasy being a making of wild sense in areas where the making of rational sense is not yet possible), and though much of it seems an exploration of bizarre dead ends, it is in fact a condition of much of their natural learning. They are not yet self-enclosed creatures. They still need to act out much of their

Sombrero and drum are part of the unexpected apparatus of education.

learning, in the form of conversation: they need to *hear* it, and to give themselves practice in formulating it. And indeed all this springs from the obvious fact that talk, and not silent thought or writing, is the medium of learning which is most natural for small children.

Our schools are not yet good enough, then, in so far as on the smallest learners they clamp too fierce a prohibition of noise and especially of general talk. And schools, except the boldest and most liberal, do tend to be against noise, and not very keen on talk: partly because of a habit schools all over the world have fallen into, and partly, it must be said, because in more schools than not there are more children in a class than is at all convenient: and teachers, even where they are not creatures of habit, are creatures to whose nervous endurance there are likely to be normal limits.

There is another truth about children and about learning that throws light on the present inadequacy of much of our schooling. Again, here is something within common experience: everyone knows how children will go dead, or become (as the adult puts it) silly, when a piece of learning is thrust upon them at the wrong moment. This is true, for example, of number. A child to whom the idea of number has as yet only a half-fantastic general meaning ('One two six ten . . . a *million*' can do service for some while) will react by going

dead, or by fooling, if the attempt is made to interest him in it, in all its strenuous detail. If the attempt is persisted with, and backed by some kind of compulsion, he will give the matter a leaden attention: but he may well acquire for number a lifelong distaste.

There is a time—and the whole agility of teaching lies in perceiving it—when children are ready for a piece of learning: and a time when they are not. Learning mechanically enforced at a sterile moment can have disastrous effects: and not always only in the sphere of that particular piece of learning—the whole morale of the child can be shaken. School, when this happens, can seem a bully, in another and worse sense—or a boor: and the child's entire impulse to learn may begin to shrink.

Now, it is true that this fact about children's learning—that there is a right moment for it and so also a wrong one—has seemed to fall into discredit, here and there. We have heard of children being forbidden to begin reading (though they are plainly eager to do so and may indeed already have begun it at home) because the first grade, or the first class, is not the place for it. But this is the mechanical reduction of an important idea to absurdity. There is no fixed *general* time for any piece of learning. The close observers of the process of learning among children, the men and women who in the

Wooden construction blocks, first brought to India by the British, are used by Tibetan refugee boys at a camp in the Himalayas.

past fifty years have built up an enormous body of patient *fact* about the development of the power to learn, have provided for our use (we make too little use of it) a great deal of certainty about this whole mysterious process. But the paradox remains: it is certainty about something essentially mysterious. It lies there, this knowledge, as a guide, a scrupulous but also a misleading guide. The Swiss-French zoologist and psychologist, Jean Piaget, than whom no one has looked with graver and more persistent closeness at the minutiae of a child's development, says on the basis of a long life of study in the Universities of Paris and Geneva that until they are eleven children cannot manage abstract ideas. The fact is that, sensitively taught, children may be at home with general scientific or mathematical concepts long before they are eleven. We don't always, and at every point, have to wait for a child to bring himself to a state of readiness: since education *is* a dialogue between teacher and taught, and the good teacher (whether he is that professionally or no) can often hasten readiness in children.

What emerges from all this is that, quite certainly, and wherever the motive comes from, a motive in the sense of a readiness for learning must be present: if it is not, then we have puzzled and mechanical pseudo-learning, which may lay a whole field of knowledge under a cloud, and may begin a process whereby the entire instinct of learning is atrophied.

I myself, as several exercise books nearly forty years old testify, somehow survived a kind of learning in which, at the age of seven, I was set each week to do something—the word is there on the page as large as life in tall childish print— called 'Transcription'. I am sure at seven no child is ready for transcription—which was, of course, the pure copying of texts from books. (It is not an activity, I think, for which anyone ought ever to be ready.) The clumsiness that set me 'transcribing' like some elderly clerk at an age when I was full willy-nilly of the raging originality of childhood must have vanished from many of the world's schools. But one doesn't have to be someone professionally given to poking his nose into schools to doubt whether such poor sense of timing, running counter to the nature of childish learning, has everywhere disappeared.

Nor has that other misconception gone that I find lies behind much of the work in those old exercise books of my own: the misconception that very early breaks the world of knowledge and skill down into separate compartments. Already, at six or seven, it may be English and Arithmetic and History and Nature Study and so on: and English may be Spelling and Dictation and Composition and Punctuation —and Literature, which even at this age may already be represented as a way of saying a plain thing in a pretty way. Unworthy of children, this hurried dismemberment of learning and knowledge! For here again, where it happens, we surely cut across the true quality of young learning: a convenience to teachers and to adults generally is a kind of impoverishment to children. To them the world is still a unity, in which all things known are yoked to all other things known, a universal network of discoveries. . . . Here is the adult, again, going wrong about children. It is the fatigued or habit-ridden adult mind that is willing to let the world of number, and space, and time and area, become 'sums': or the gorgeous vegetable world become 'Nature Study'.

I remember, as an illustration, that one of my own sons, stunned at the age of five by the revelation that the wide world of fields, plants, trees and stones was properly to be regarded as 'Nature Study', would spend much of his free time collecting leaves and acorns and moss and laying them out on his 'nature table'. 'Have you seen my *nature*, Dad?' he would inquire: and once he came in from the garden carrying some soil-covered mystery and asked, 'Mum, is *this* nature?'

It may be just as much a shrinkage of the child mind when the big cosmic questions are reduced at school to pieties. Under the impact of Religious Instruction, the five-year-old in our house said to the three-year-old, to end a quarrel, 'Jesus will forgive you.' He filled the house with the inaccurate bawling of hymns, and to his mother's horror clapped his hands together in the middle of a shopping expedition and prayed most ostentatiously.

Of course, structure there must be: by the time they are seven or eight most healthy and happy children will have created for themselves a simple framework of concepts that will make the world—at any rate, the world of *things*— manageable to them. It is a matter of how they acquire this structure: whether it is through a delicate and imaginative commerce with the adult mind, or whether it is through some sort of clumsy and possibly incompetent imposition. (The use by teachers of the word 'area', for example, in place of the carefully organized practical experience of area, can be petrifying to children: and indeed in their exchanges with children adults have to be most careful in their use of words. To an adult a word may be a summation of much experience: to a child it may be as blank as the moon. And words, for the very young, slide into other words: for a long time one of my sons believed that the jackets worn by English schoolchildren were called *razors*. I always count it as an unlikely triumph of my own that, being confronted in one of my first reading books with a picture of a grinning teapot, and under it the word 'coun-ten-ance', I knew at once that this word referred to the grin, and was not a synonym for 'teapot'.)

The way in which children move best towards constructing their earliest intellectual framework is well understood. They build on knowledge they already have, and securely have. They learn by making and doing, by discovering how things work or what causes them not to work, by establishing or having made clear to them the conditions of success in any field, by the constant activity of comparing and arranging, of marshalling the world's objects into distinct classes, by hitting upon similarities and pinning down differences.

Such a list is easy to draw up, but in fact to act on our understanding that this is the intellectual way of things among children isn't at all simple. I can't have been, theoretically, so ignorant of childish nature as was suggested by my behaviour as a young untrained teacher. I addressed my first class, on the basis of voluminous and carefully prepared notes, as if they had been around for thirty years or more, and during that time had been doing little but study. The spokesman of their rebellion, struggling for a formula for what they all felt, came out with what, in the circumstances, was a courteous inquiry: 'Sir,' he asked, 'are you a teacher?' I wasn't. I had forgotten what it was like to be in the marvellous foothills of learning, where everything was still to be charted.

But the drive, certainly, among children, is towards order and organization: towards making the chart. And here lies the danger for the adult, be he parent or teacher or whatever: he is easily tempted to impose notions of organization, abstractly (why not 'area' as a quick shorthand?); he is easily led to break down the world of knowledge—social and emotional as well as intellectual knowledge—only too manageably. And children may seem to drive the adult in this direction, since they need to create a framework as a defence against helplessness and dread of the unknown, the *unplaced* or *unplaceable*.

The secret lies, surely, in as much sensitiveness as possible on the part of the adult, who must think of his task as one of collaboration with the young mind: not dictatorial, but immensely observant: helping to bring order about, but not at the expense of richness or—to use an old sentimental word that is difficult to replace—at the expense of wonder. How far he is still from doing this, in general, in the world's schools, can be seen from an examination of the typical early reading book, with its dull respectability of vocabulary and themes. Why should small children have to read about conventional hens in conventional farmyards, or about the polite acts of generalized children called Jack and Jill, when they might make their own reading books, using words that arise out of their own ungeneralized needs, and that treat of the actual people and the actual life around and within them? The need is to root learning in what they specifically are, as particular children: for this only will prevent learning from becoming an abstraction, departing further and further from the warm centre of experience: something against which, as they advance towards their teens, they have begun to acquire the habit of struggling.

All these problems, of matching the passion for learning in young children with a kind of schooling that will do it justice, arise in sophisticated areas of the world, or in areas where the march towards sophistication has begun. In primitive cultures, where so much less has to be attempted within enclosed traditions smoothed with time, the progress of the young to adulthood by way of learning seems much happier. There will be a time when the mother is mentor, and there will be established pieces of learning—simple domestic learning largely—for which she is responsible. There are age grades, and it is well understood what learning will occur during each grade. Moral education may be given by way of traditional stories: the avoidance of quarrelling, the giving of honour where honour is due, the need to work hard and to run an errand quickly—these may be the pieces of learning acquired as you squat eagerly round the storyteller in the moonlight. Some member of the family acts as your tutor in the matter of local history, or language, or in the techniques of farming. Ceremonies punctuate your progress: you know the point you have reached in your growing up—the stage of learning you are at. It is all warmed by its intimate family nature: it is always related to *you* because this is preparation for *your* life: it exists comfortably within the framework of a simple set of traditions. The connection between life and learning is always obvious.

There is no going back from sophistication. In advanced parts of the world we could, presumably, simplify a great many of the problems of growing up if we still had initiation ceremonies that made it clear exactly at what point a boy had become a man and a girl a woman. But there is no going back. I've often thought, though, that just as the highly sophisticated artist has glanced behind him at primitive art in order to refresh and restore his sense of the very nature of art, so sophisticated adults might look back at primitive forms of education for certain principles of which we so often lose sight—among them the simple, often repeated but still all too rarely practised notion that we should try to match the richness of a child's eagerness for learning by keeping it close to the generous inquisitive warmth of childish nature.

Perhaps, where children are concerned, it's the word *learning* itself that we've allowed to become soured. It is extraordinary to remember that children were once taught—and so *learned*—to walk. Today—it's the only way to put it—they get so that they find out how to walk. It's a learning process, in fact, but perhaps it's nowadays one of the generally happy and successful pieces of learning because, simply by trusting to our belief that it's something children *want* to do, we've forgotten that it's something to be learned.

**'And then the whining schoolboy, with his satchel
And shining morning face, creeping like snail
Unwillingly to school.'**
—William Shakespeare

Properly dressed and properly perched on a luggage van, this English boy now has nothing left to do but wait to be shipped off to his boarding school. His shining morning face is twisted with indifference, his eyes heavy with boredom, his stiff upper lip slightly less than stiff.

Proper dress is not one of the worries of the Aborigine children who pad stark naked alongside their mother on the opening day of their mission school in Australia. When their curiosity has been satisfied, perhaps they too will creep unwillingly, but today, the first day, brings only great adventure.

Uniform education

William Wordsworth and the Romantics liked to regard formal education as the systematized corruption of innocence and natural piety by the grimy world. Whether they were wrong or right it is true that the very young are not naturally suited to discipline and to introduce them to books and lessons is, for better or worse, to put them in a straight jacket. One of the most useful devices for achieving scholarly unanimity is the school uniform, whether it be a polka dot jumper or an Eton collar. Uniforms also make small scholars easier to keep track of in the streets.

Top-hatted choristers of King's College Choir School march across the quadrangle at Canterbury, England.

Girls in polka dots cling dutifully together so as not to be separated from the group as an elementary school class parades through Sofia on its way to a museum.

Barefoot boys in bonnets and girlish smocks at Nazare, Portugal.

The Universal Passport

Every day school becomes a more universally accepted part of life in every corner of the world. 'Education' covers a multitude of activities from nature study in scholarly ranks in Nigeria to self-expressing free play at a Sunday School in Philadelphia. But whatever education is, it is generally agreed that everyone has a right to it. In America the original conception of the equality of men included the equal right to education as its first principle. In quantity, if not necessarily in quality, America is now pressing close to the achievement of universal education. In Nigeria, as in other newly independent countries, schooling regardless of content is blindly viewed as a passport to employment and affluence.

Showing that you know

Statistics are depressing. In Pakistan only nineteen per cent of the people are literate. In Iran, even with all sorts of new programmes, schooling is open to only sixty-six per cent of all children.

But when you're at the blackboard with everyone watching or desperately scratching your head for an answer, the problem is not statistical but personal. Tests, everywhere, are a challenge and a threat. Unfortunately, as literacy increases, the importance of testing to success in life also seems to increase, a fact just as depressing as the worst statistics.

At a loss for an answer in history, an English boy stands before his class, hoping perhaps to be rescued from humiliation by an interruption—like the disturbance made by the boy in the foreground flicking a pellet at a friend with his ruler.

A teenage Iranian girl, in Teheran, chalks out an answer naturally from right to left.

Boys learning Urdu in an open-air class at Lahore, Pakistan, write answers on clay-covered boards which can be wiped clean like slates.

The Class Society

New faces and new shoes. The restless assembly (below) is a Paris kindergarten at the beginning of term. It is also the beginning of a new society. In the hands of a capable teacher these children will soon have something more in common than restlessness—like the adoring pre-school group in Philadelphia (left) and the tiny attentive class in Bengal (below, left).

Putting pen to paper

'Don't you remember the first time you were given a pencil and tried to write? And how fascinated you were at first by the fact that you could manage to make scribbles all over the paper? Finally it became much more satisfying to do something *deliberate* all over the paper. Then came strokes and letters.'
—Erna Wright in *The New Childbirth*

Girl in Karachi with pencil and clay-covered board. In London, girl with brush and paper.

The trappings of history

They don't realize it yet, but they are surrounded by history. And some day soon they will suddenly discover that just by being involved in the process of learning they have become part of a community of scholars that stretches back for centuries.

But for the present, the public school crests on the wall of the Hall School in Hampstead, London, are only unnoticed accompaniments to food.

And in Leningrad young players concentrate on their game, oblivious to the beauties of the Young Pioneers' Palace, which was once owned by a favourite count of Catherine the Great.

The lighter side of lower learning

The boy at left seems to be industriously bent on separating himself from one of his fingers. Surrounded by all the accoutrements of higher learning the junior scholar at right is gravely making a valedictorian's speech at a kindergarten graduation ceremony in Detroit, Michigan. The two little girls in attitudes of extreme piety only slightly marred by a yawn are dutifully saying grace in London. But preposterous as it sometimes seems, the process of simply trying to act like adults is part of education.

Apprentices to life

For these children, Australian natives in Northern Arnhem Land and an Indian boy at Benares, academic training is a long way off.

The aboriginal children receive no official schooling. What they learn, they learn from their parents. Their father is showing them how to skin a blue-tongued lizard which will be cooked in a fire lighted with flint.

The Indian boy is already at work as an apprentice to a weaver.

'The man that hath not music in himself,
Nor is not moved with concord of sweet sounds,
Is fit for treasons, stratagems, and spoils.'
—William Shakespeare

In Ghana, after the official police-band practice, the sons of Accra policemen (left) cheerfully swing out in an impromptu jam session, accompanied by a small, one-man rhythm-section on the side. Below, in America, an overdressed angel in a school Nativity play tortuously conjures notes from his violin. But whether painfully formal or free-and-easily informal, music is clearly a prime instrument of pleasure, harmony and civilization.

Expansion vs concentration

In a class to encourage movement and free expression to music at Rollesborn, England, small girls give way to satisfyingly large gestures of utter delight and/or despair.

Rehearsing for a school orchestra, a boy concentrates on the intense discipline imposed by a musical score and the beat of an imaginary metronome.

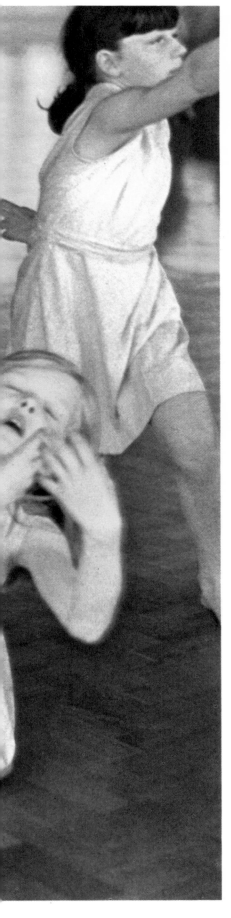

91

The book of nature

The little New Zealand girl absorbs the lessons of the fields while accompanying her father as he herds his sheep in the shadow of Mount Cook.

The Brazilian Indian children of the Karajá tribe make a practical study of the ways of nature. Living near the Araguaia river in the jungle of the Amazon basin, they become highly skilled at shooting fish with a bow and arrow.

Art and imitation

Whether an expression of artistic will
or a simple act of mimicry, learning to
do something with your hands is the
beginning of a cycle of learning from
which sculptors, tailors and designers
may develop.

England: a formal modelling class at
Leicester.

South Africa: sidewalk sculptors in
Johannesburg.

94

France: a housewifely gesture to smooth a handkerchief for ironing.

Sweden: a small boy sticks to his knitting.

Wisdom: inquiry or acceptance?

For these Bulgarian children (below) whose family is dependent on tobacco, copying the way their parents link the green leaves together to dry them for the market is really the placid acceptance of a way of life. Much practical learning, like theirs, can only be acquired by unthinkingly doing what has always been done, and accepting the role one is expected to play.

But there is another sort of education that can only begin by questioning the value of things as they are, of worldly life as it is habitually lived. The four Burmese boys (opposite) standing contemplatively before a splendid golden Buddhist temple are novice monks, already embarked on a spiritual inquiry which will last throughout their lifetimes.

Playing

'The child's toys and the old man's reasons are the fruits of the two seasons'
—William Blake

Pure reason and pure play have more in common than most people realize. Both are activities which modern society has long thought it could do without. Generated by a spirit of challenge to the demands of the 'real world', both have been considered inappropriate to the practical business of adult life.

Rolling a bicycle tyre through a Saigon street just before eleven p.m. (opposite) doesn't help the war effort. It is, besides, a challenge to the curfew. The hoop is one of many playthings which used to be enjoyed by grown-ups as well as children. Explaining why this is no longer so, Philippe Ariès, the French author of *Centuries of Childhood*, in the first part of the following chapter traces the development of games through the Industrial Revolution, when work drove out play and old games, once played in common, began to be looked down on as mere 'child's play'.

Today, adults with more leisure again, are returning to games for recreation, and 'child's play' has become 'the means above all others by which children reduce the world to manageable proportions and find their place in it.' This definition is from Phyllis Hostler, British child psychologist, who, in the second part of this chapter, discusses play as the child's means of mastering reality—an intellectual exercise not very different from the old man's reasoning.

But anyone who has ever watched a child sliding, swinging, or throwing pebbles on a beach, knows that play is more than a challenge, more than a game, more than therapeutic imitation. This special quality is what led Schiller to say 'Man is human only when he plays.'

Games, fashions and society

Philippe Ariès
Translated from the French by Robert Baldick

In our Western civilization, down to the eighteenth century at least, the words 'games' and 'play' did not suggest anything childish. They formed part of the vocabulary of adults, and the activities they described were common to both adults and children, partly because both groups shared in the same ceremonies, partly because the notion of children as a separate group to be worried about and treated differently from adults did not exist.

The relegation of games mainly to children is a modern development closely related to a great many changes that have taken place both in the nature of childhood itself and our conceptions of it. The famous Dutch psychologist, Meneer Van den Berg was quite right when he said, 'The child has not always been a child: he has become one. The child only appears a child in comparison with what is not childish, that is to say, in comparison with things which are adult.' In the days when everyone played games and children were expected to take a great share of adult work there was little distinction between adults and children, but when the need for children to work dropped off and play became a less important part of the adult world too, play became a more important part of the child's world—and both worlds moved into self-conscious 'age groups'.

The oldest, truest and most functional form of play was the ceremonial festival. At least as old as civilization itself, the festival has always been a time when members of the village community gathered together to renew its mystical unity by taking part in a series of ritual activities. During these times, ordinary life and work were suspended, and sometimes, too, the normal roles and hierarchies of ordinary life were turned upside down (as on Candlemas, when the *men* made the pancakes). Such goings-on were not regarded as mere relaxation, but as a ceremony essential to the continuity of the group.

Children took part in these festivals on an equal footing with all the other members of society, though because of their size they naturally often played roles which were suited to them physically and, as a result, came to be reserved for them.

Twelfth Night (the twelfth after Christmas), the greatest of the seasonal festivals which crowded the calendar of pre-industrial Europe, consisted of several episodes. The first was the sharing-out of the Twelfth-cake, an operation which was carried out in accordance with a set formula. Traditionally, a child hid under the table; then one of the guests cut the cake, calling out, '*Phoebe, domine*' at every slice. From under the table the child replied each time by giving the name of the guest to be served.

The second episode was the toast drunk to the guest who had found the traditional bean in his portion of the cake and had thus become the 'bean king'. The entire company gathered round the king—old people, grown men, women and children, with the young men in fancy dress. This company was the whole social group—family, relatives, neighbours, friends—without any distinctions of sex and age.

After the drinking came the vigil which lasted until morning. One of the guests, dressed as a buffoon, led a little procession consisting largely of young men, some of them masked, others playing the fiddle, and finally a child, probably the child who had shared out the Twelfth-cake, who always

carried the many-coloured candle of the kings. The procession, known in France as 'the singers of the star', paraded through the winter darkness knocking at the doors of neighbouring farms and houses, where they were invited in and given food and drink.

Other festivals, though still concerning the entire community, gave youth the monopoly of the active roles while everyone else looked on as spectators. On the Feast of the Holy Innocents, celebrated on December 28, the church was given over completely to children. One was elected bishop, and he conducted a service which continued with a procession. A collection was taken, and the whole celebration finished with a banquet at which the proceeds of the collection were eaten—and drunk.

The Carnival just before Lent, which still exists, of course, was the greatest holiday for youth. It was organized by a leader variously known as the Prince of Love, the King of the Clerks, the Abbot or Captain of Youth. Adolescents played the chief parts putting on fancy dress for evening parties, acting out farces (*charivari*) in which cuckolded husbands and widowers who had remarried were ridiculed. There were also games in which the players threw firebrands—lighted branches—into the air, at the same time announcing marriages, revealing love-affairs, and linking the names of couples. The fun was in the indiscretions. A festival of love, of fertility? Yes, but also a festival of students, young and old.

Thomas à Becket's English biographer tells us how Shrove Tuesday, the highlight of Carnival, was spent in the twelfth century, at the cathedral school of St Paul's in London: 'All the schoolchildren brought their fighting-cocks to their master.' The cockfighting lasted all morning. 'In the afternoon, the young people of the town went into the outskirts for the famous ball game. . . . The adults, relatives and notables came on horseback to watch the young people's games and to become young again with them.'

Two of the festivals in which children played a large part were those which occurred in May and November: May Day and what nowadays is Hallowe'en. On May Day children were crowned with garlands of flowers and went from door to door. Everyone was supposed to give them something to eat in return for their good wishes. This custom of wreathing children with flowers must have been associated with the idea of rebirth implicit in spring buds and blossoming. This idea was reinforced, too, by the may-tree (later to become the maypole) which children carried through the streets of the town and then planted.

House-to-house collections were one of the essential elements of May Day and the other festivals of youth. This custom has survived in America as the 'trick-or-treat' of Hallowe'en, a holiday which was originally a masquerade for young people, and not simply children. At the end of the sixteenth century this festival was held near the beginning of November, shortly after All Souls' Day. However, public opinion refused to allow a joyful masquerade to follow so closely on such a solemn day, and the festival all but disappeared from the calendars of Europe.

In all festivals of this kind, the most active part was played by the young—a group in which children and what we think

of as adolescents were mingled together. In France the word
enfant was used until the eighteenth century to describe
children of sixteen or eighteen as well as those of six or seven.
But the very fact that different roles in these festivals were
traditionally played by different age groups suggests that there
was once a division of society itself into age groups, divisions
which were preserved in the games and ceremonies even when
they no longer existed in society. The character of popular
games and festivals is always conservative: they prolong and
preserve customs whose origin and function have both been
long forgotten.

Children mixed with adults not only during public rituals
and festivals, but also privately, at home, in parlour games and
amusements. This lasted as long as entertainment was
primarily something a family had to provide for itself. When
professional entertainment grew widespread, family games
declined along with such skills as the ability to sing acceptably
before company. Naturally, at family parties, the activities of
children were very similar to the activities of adults. They
joined adults in playing chamber music and sang in the choirs
which performed on all occasions. They also took part in balls,
especially in the ballet interludes—which were not danced by
professionals at all until the end of the seventeenth century.

Children's round dances copied the dances of adults in
every particular. At the age of three, Louis XIII danced the
galliard, the saraband and the old bourrée like a young man.
At four, he practised archery and took part in the physical
games of strength and skill which were played by adults. He
played tennis at the same time as he played with dolls.
Stranger still, to our modern minds, at the age of five he was
playing cards, which were then simply games of chance
played for money. When he was eight he won a jewel at
blanque—a game comparable with those played in modern
casinos—at which large sums were gambled and fortunes were
made and lost. A seventeenth-century engraving by the
painter Stella shows a *putto* in the depths of despair because
he has lost all his money at dice, and the Caravaggian painters
of the same period often show children barely ten years old
playing excitedly in low taverns, surrounded by villainous-
looking soldiers.

Conversely, adults played games which we would nowadays
reserve for children. The company at the Hôtel de Ram-
bouillet, which was the intellectual centre of the best Parisian
society during the first half of the seventeenth century, used
to play blind man's buff. Sixteenth-century tapestries and
seventeenth-century Dutch paintings are full of games like
hot cockles and hide-and-seek in which there are sometimes a
sprinkling of children, mingled with the mass of grown-up
players. The modern observer cannot fail to be struck by this
unity of the age groups.

The dolls, the scale models, the 'little German cabinets'—
all ancestors of today's children's toys—also appealed to adult
tastes. Grown-ups collected, and played with, all sorts of toys
and knick-knacks: tiny sedan chairs, miniature coffee and
chocolate services, little scenes peopled by beribboned shep-
herds in porcelain, not to mention complicated reproductions
of dwelling-houses, presented like modern stage-sets, with
their various floors, rooms and pieces of furniture, inhabited

The maypole, which was once a may-tree, still provides enjoyment at a children's festival in Western Australia.

by pug dogs and tiny dolls painted and dressed correctly in every detail.

Dolls were collected by adults as amusing objects, but they had other uses as well. During the seventeenth century, when fashion was beginning to change more and more frequently, dolls served as fashion models which were sent to elegant women to show them the latest designs.

Adults and children shared many games and pastimes, festivals and toys for a long time. But by the early sixteenth century, signs began to appear of a contrary trend which eventually ended in today's system, in which age groups are totally divided. Adults of the upper classes began separating themselves both from the lower classes and from their own children. In the poorer classes, the old mingling of grown-ups and children lasted much longer.

The effect on games was predictable. Festivals, toys and amusements abandoned by the adult world more and more became the province and property of children. Usually the games and festivals became simpler, easier and less sumptuous. This, at any rate, was the fate of even the great medieval tournaments and duels of chivalry. Tournaments were abandoned at the end of the sixteenth century and replaced

with games which tested the skill of the riders playing them. An example was tilting at the quintain: the player had to knock over with his lance the wooden target painted as a Turk's head in memory of the Crusades. The wooden head took the place of the living adversary of the tournaments. Another game which originated in the age of chivalry was tilting at the ring: the player had to catch a ring with his lance while riding at full gallop. Neither tilting at the quintain nor tilting at the ring have any place at horse-shows today. All the same, they have not entirely disappeared: at French fairgrounds today, contestants still throw wooden balls to knock down Turks' heads, and until a few years ago, the owners of merry-go-rounds used to challenge children to catch hold of a ring while the merry-go-round was moving.

Fairground throwing contests and merry-go-rounds—this is what has become of the aristocratic games which were played at the court of the Bourbons, the games which had been, in turn, derived from great tournaments of the age of chivalry. Games, like toys and festivals, took refuge with the children, who shared them with the adults of the lower classes. The common people and children became, in fact, unwitting preservers of the old customs which had long since been cast off by grown-ups of the upper classes.

Football is one of the many games which changed hands like this. At the time of Henry VIII, kings did not scorn the challenge of a rough game. King Henri II of France played football. But the ball game, rough in nature, soon became suspect to experts on etiquette and good manners. James I of England forbade his sons to kick a ball around, and Shakespeare warned noblemen against it. In France by the seventeenth century the game was no longer played by anyone but the peasants.

Consider, as well, the case of the fairy tale. These extraordinary romantic stories were born of an old folk tradition and of the courtly literature of the Middle Ages. Some people read them, many told them in company at sophisticated gatherings. Colbert, the great finance minister of Louis XIV, employed servants whose sole job was to tell him fairy tales during his rare moments of leisure.

People of all ages enjoyed fairy tales. Eighteenth-century hawkers in France, at least, sold small volumes full of fairy tales—known as the Blue Library. Professional storytellers, heirs of the old entertainers of the Middle Ages, told the same tales aloud in village squares.

But by the eighteenth century the aristocracy in the big towns, and later in the country, had stopped gathering together to listen to such storytellers. Fairy stories and courtly romances went on filling the pages of the Blue Library, but eventually, in the nineteenth century, even the poorer classes lost interest in them, too, leaving only the children to be amused by Red Riding Hood and Cinderella. Nowadays even the children have begun neglecting them in favour of other tales inspired by more modern subjects: spies or gangsters, war, the wild west and men from Mars.

Whether the declining popularity of fairy stories is the result of a continuing corruption of taste or increased sophistication is a moot point. But it is tolerably clear why games once common to all age-groups were slowly abandoned by adults and left to children. The cause was a change in the conception of play and the function of games which developed during the early stages of the Industrial Revolution. It was at this time that the value of play, amusement and recreation began to disappear. Work became the essential value of capitalistic society, and play occupied a humble position at best. Only when reserved for the young was it accepted as an activity that was useful and respectable. Games were no longer semi-sacred rituals involving the entire community. They were no longer essential demonstrations which had a regenerating

Fairy tales used to be written for everyone. Now they are part of a vast literature exclusively for children.

effect. They were no longer played by all age-groups and all classes. And finally, they were no longer played in a special period of time, set apart from, and above, everyday life, during which ordinary life was deliberately turned topsy-turvy, its prohibitions defied and its restrictions suspended.

Once they had been reserved for children, games became the object of a process of moral selection. Games of chance, for instance, once common to all age groups, were now regarded as no longer suitable for children. In the eighteenth century there had appeared in English a new word, 'gambling', in place of the more general term 'gaming', as if at that time a stricter distinction was being made between games of chance and the rest, which were nearly all children's games; naturally this trend increased during the Victorian Age. In *Tom Brown's Schooldays*, written by Thomas Hughes in 1857, it was regarded as scandalous that students at Rugby should make bets on the Derby. Of course, this censorious attitude has not prevented children from continuing, among themselves, to play games like 'odds or evens', with marbles hidden in clenched fists.

Adults had now taken control of children's games: play was no longer left either to tradition or individual initiative. Games now belonged to the realm not of amusement but of formal instruction and this was a significant and in some ways a depressing change. In the civilizations of ancient Greece and Rome, games and athletic exercises formed an integral part of a child's education, and were co-ordinated with strictly academic studies. This co-ordination disappeared in the Middle Ages, because of the essentially clerical character of medieval education. On the one hand, there was the profane world, with its ritual festivals, its games, its explosions of gaiety, its mockery of society; and on the other hand, the world of serious, moralizing people, missionaries of order and reason. These people tended to condemn all games, whatever their character, as undisciplined, crude, regressive activities. College statutes in the late Middle Ages prohibited nearly all games, barely tolerating tennis. Needless to say, these prohibitions were not observed, games went on being played with delight. But the warnings and restrictions were nonetheless patiently repeated.

By the late sixteenth and early seventeenth centuries all this had changed. The Jesuits in particular began to recognize the educational possibilities of games, and introduced them into their schools—even the most questionable games, like play-acting and ballet-dancing. Dancing was thought to give a boy poise, a good bearing, a 'fine air'.

The Jesuits were also among the first to see the value of educational gymnastics. They wrote Latin treatises on gymnastics, possibly the first of their kind, which included rules for recommended games chosen for the sake of their physical activity. Races, leapfrog, prisoners' base, and tag, which were played in the fifteenth century by noble lords and gentle ladies, now became purely physical gymnastic exercises.

By the end of the seventeenth century, games were used informally as models for teaching the chronology of the kings of France and the names of countries. But the serious technique of teaching with games developed only during the eighteenth century, particularly under the influence of the ideas of Jean-Jacques Rousseau, who based his educational theory on the doctrine of the return to nature. He believed the child's early training should avoid verbal lessons, logic, books and strict discipline, and should concentrate instead on the development of the heart and intelligence by sympathy and example, so as to produce spontaneous good behaviour. Under Rousseau's influence, Madame de Genlis brought up the children of the Duc d'Orléans in such a way that not a single moment was wasted: there was no amusement without instruction, no game without profit. Even a stroll was used to count the trees which lined the streets or rows of flower-pots on a terrace.

This new order, in which children were more and more isolated from other social groups and games were reserved for them as a necessary part of education, was for a long time confined to the rich middle classes and the aristocracy. During the eighteenth and nineteenth centuries the middle classes grew steadily more numerous and influential, and middle-class methods of bringing up children eventually spread, with mass education, to lower-class families.

The development of mass education is undoubtedly the most important social change that has ever taken place. And its roots may be older than is generally thought, if they can be dated back to the time when children began to form a market for the products of the new industrial age.

The 'children's market' was born in the middle of the eighteenth century, with the beginning of the specialized publication of children's books. In the seventeenth and early eighteenth centuries a rich pedagogical literature *about* children existed, even though there were as yet no books intended solely *for* children. Fairy stories and courtly romances, like Perrault's fairy tales, had been reserved for them when adults had stopped reading them. But these were stories which children shared with the common people, and which had not been written specifically for them. In France the great pioneer was Arnaud Berquin who died in 1791, and whose works in the 1803 edition comprised twenty volumes, under the title of *The Village Library, the Children's Friend*. François Fréville, another lesser-known French author of the same period, named one of his sons Emile, after the hero of Rousseau's great educational treatise. Emile died at the age of seven, and his unhappy father wrote *The Life and Republican Death of Little Emilien* for the edification of the little children of the revolutionary era. His masterpiece, *The Lives of Famous Children*, which was reprinted many times, told again of little

Emilien, recounted the sad life of Louis XVI's son, who died in prison at the age of ten, and praised the child heroes of classical antiquity. These, the first books for children, were above all educational. But writers of children's books later became imaginative. In the second half of the nineteenth century most of the books which are now regarded as classic works of children's literature were written.

For a long time children, though they formed a new reading public, were thought to be without any purchasing power of their own. They were a public reached through parents or teachers. But after the Second World War this group was largely set free of the control of family and school. Publishers of books and periodicals, writers of songs, and record and toy manufacturers now address themselves directly to children as well as continuing to approach them, as in the past, through their parents and teachers. Children and adolescents are recognized as a separate group with individual tastes. Modern techniques of promotion and distribution are very often aimed directly at them.

This great change which we have lately witnessed is still taking place. From the eighteenth century to the beginning of the twentieth century, school-children, who were submitted to a rigid, authoritarian education, were a group apart from the rest of society. During the twentieth century the length of childhood and the attitude of adults toward leisure have altered again. Under the influence of the continued prolongation of schooling and extension of the school-leaving age, as the growing reluctance on the part of families to let their children go out into life too soon, a long period has established itself between a childhood whose frontier is indefinite, and adult life—the strange period known as adolescence. So persuasive are the signs of adolescence today that it is almost impossible to believe the condition did not formerly exist. Children went straight from childhood to adult life.

But once adolescence was created it was clearly impossible to treat adolescents in the same way as children. A long series of attempts was made to satisfy their restlessness, enterprise and sociability, and at the same time to channel those energies constructively. This was the object of the Boy Scout movement, which began in Britain in 1908. Its aim was to compensate for the prolonged seclusion which came with longer periods of schooling, and to bring young men closer to the natural world from which modern life was separating them. Adolescence was regarded as the period when relaxation and contact with nature were still possible, before the adult's irrevocable involvement in industrial and urban civilization began. Games therefore became the reconstruction of uncivilized life in a natural environment, on the pattern of Red Indians or jungle children. They were no longer imitations of adult society, but images of the opposite of that society.

Today the young increasingly refuse to accept the planned leisure which adults offer them. They form their own society with its own rules, and coalesce in spontaneous organizations known as 'gangs'. It is the gang which the adolescent asks to occupy his spare time, to satisfy his desire for fellowship, and also to initiate him into adult life, at a time when the passage to the state of adulthood is more difficult and demanding than ever before. Adolescent pastimes now are naturally imitations of adult life, but altered, distorted, exaggerated: games which are meant to be men's games, games with motorcycles and real cars, sex games, games of violence which sometimes go as far as criminal assault.

The Victorian moralistic attitude of serious adult society towards leisure has changed radically in the twentieth century. Leisure has ceased to be something shameful, and there is now a recognized need for recreation. J. Dumazedier, an eminent French sociologist of leisure, has pointed out that nineteenth-century dictionaries defined leisure as time left available after work, and that those of the twentieth century add another meaning: 'Distractions and occupations in which one indulges one's own free will during the time which is not taken up by ordinary work.'

Leisure is occupying an ever-increasing place in consumer societies, where the search for the satisfaction of basic needs has been replaced by the search for 'the good life'. Games have to some extent recovered the place in adult life which they lost during the first part of the Industrial Revolution. Some traditional games which had been more or less abandoned are being played by everybody again. There is nothing more extraordinary in this respect than the present success of bowls in France. Bowls used to be played all over France, but during the industrial era the game had been relegated to the south-east, and people regarded it as essentially Provençal, the pastime of easy-going southerners. Now, emerging from its retreat in Provence, it has recaptured the whole of France— beaches, village squares, city parks, and suburban backyards.

The twentieth century has created its own toys. The car, life-size, is an adult's toy, and in miniature a child's toy, but the child is fascinated by his father's big car, while the father has time to amuse himself collecting little children's cars.

Finally there is the almost universal absorption in television. But how many adults stop looking at the little screen when programmes specially intended for children and young people begin? And how many young people are prevented from watching programmes which are not meant for them?

This rapprochement of the family in the car on Sundays, or in front of the television screen, does not mean that the barriers are down between the different age groups. Far from it, for frequent tensions explode far more dangerously in these more restricted circumstances. But parents and children *are* beginning to join more often in the same games. A mixed zone has been created between the age groups which have been kept apart since the eighteenth century.

Children and adults have not yet returned to the unified group of the old pre-industrial civilization. Such a unity would be impossible just now, when the world of the adolescent has only recently been discovered and is still being defined. For, while the adolescent may drive a man's car or a man's motorcycle, and play men's games, he refuses to imitate his elders. He no longer tries to look older in order to give the impression that he is ready to enter the adult world, as was the case not very long ago. He has forgotten the children's games of old, and he has adopted men's games once more, but he turns his back on the adult world and refuses to enter it.

Play with a purpose

Phyllis Hostler

'This is the pigs' food,' says the four-year-old, rapidly tearing green toffee paper to shreds. '*There you are, piggies!—good piggies!—eat it all up, that's right! Now I'm going to take you to market to be killed!—in the truck you go! Honk, honk, brrr, brrr!—off they go! And the little baby pig can stay here with his mummy, and have the pen all to himself. . . .*'

An adult may react to child's play of this kind with amusement, enjoyment and interest, or irritation and plain puzzlement. Much will depend on the adult's temperament—perhaps, also on whether the child is his own or not. But the more mature we are, the more sympathy and understanding we shall feel, and the less inclined we shall be to shrug off the reality of the child's world, so different from our own.

If today more and more people are able to achieve this tolerance and empathy as regards children, it is modern psychological theory that has made this possible.

The pioneers were in one sense those great enough to become themselves, so to speak, *as little children*. Jean-Jacques Rousseau brought a new idea to mothers of the upper classes when he urged them to suckle their infants and to bring them up within the haven of the family circle. Jean Marc Gaspard Itard, at the beginning of the nineteenth century, discovered a wild young boy who had been found roaming in the woods like an animal, tamed him through love, and taught him by means of play and games. Friedrich Froebel urged that children be given employment 'in keeping with their whole nature' and thought of a school as a garden (*Kindergarten*) in which they could grow. Maria Montessori introduced her 'sense-training apparatus'—toys that teach concepts of shape, size, colour. Sigmund Freud toppled the idea that a child is a *tabula rasa*, a clean slate on which adults might write what they pleased, and replaced it with the notion of the rich and urgent life of the unconscious which incessantly drives children forward into conflict with the 'reality principle' that governs social living.

The theories and insights of these and others have led to a conglomerate mass of knowledge about the nature of children's play rather than to a systematic presentation of facts. This is because in the very nature of psychology each new discovery bears the mark of its maker—as Freud's teaching bears the imprint of his Jewish background with its tyrannical Jehovah. But though so many minds have been at work, each with its own characteristic colouring, the interweaving of those minds has produced a stuff that seems likely to endure: the texture is firm, the colours harmonious.

All the theorists, to begin with, are agreed on the fundamental importance of the role of children's play in the development of personality. This importance is most effectively summarized in the words of Susan Isaacs, the English child psychologist: 'Play is supremely the activity which brings the child psychic equilibrium in the early years.' It is only after long hours of varied play that a child can come to terms with the world he must live in, find out about himself and his environment and learn to accept his own limitations and those that are imposed on him.

Why should this be so? Why, in the normal loving home where a child's needs are satisfied as fully as may be, with food, clothes, warmth, toys, interest and sympathy at his command,

should a child need play so desperately? Why can't play simply be regarded as a wholesome method of filling up time, a means of getting the child into the fresh air, giving him a break from school and a chance to let off steam? The answer is that, while play certainly does do all these things it does much more. It remains the means above all others by which children reduce the world to manageable proportions, and find their place in it.

It is through play, first of all, that a baby makes the major and exhilarating discovery of his own separateness. As early as twelve weeks, his hands swim into his field of vision. He examines them as curiously as the rattle pinned to the hood of his pram, watches them open and shut like flowers. But he begins dimly to understand that they actually *belong to him* only when they get tangled in his shawl and must be set free. His toes are not his own until by accident he bites them and cries out in astonished pain. But other areas of his body yield him pleasure—his thumb through sucking, his genitals through fondling. These are his very first toys, and it is through this earliest play that he builds up, by exploration and experiment, an image of his own body.

Then play brings power. He slaps his heels down hard and feels the water in the bathtub spraying over him in fountains. His hands, he discovers, are tools: he shakes his rattle, drops it, finds it again, sucks it, throws it out of the cot, watches his mother bend down to retrieve it. He raises his head, turns it from side to side, covers his face with the coverlet, pushes it down to make the world come back. Then he is on the floor, and suddenly no longer needs to cry for his ball—he can get it for himself. Soon his mother cannot escape either. He can run after her, and even climb the stairs at her heels.

Mastery of his top-heavy body comes quickly. Toddlers begin to climb up a stair or two and then jump down or mount a whole flight, turn over on their faces and slide safely to the bottom. The four-year-old boy playing so busily with his 'pig-farm', has learned to tuck himself into a neat, compact mass so that he can move his arms freely, see what he is doing, reach out without overbalancing, pick up half-inch animals, open and close a tiny door on a toy truck with a fastening no bigger than a pin-head. By the time he is seven he will stand teetering on the top of a fence and, arms flailing to keep him there, will judge precisely the second when he may jump.

But at every level in this quest through play for physical independence, for some new assertion of his power to 'do it by himself', he is dogged at every twist and turn by proofs of his powerlessness. His clumsy grasp knocks over every tower he builds. No sooner has he learned to pick up each brick neatly with finger and thumb than he finds that the same finger and thumb are not strong enough to turn the key of his clockwork car. With great effort, he can pull himself up to play with the beads on the side of his play pen, but, try as he will, the doll on top of the chest-of-drawers remains out of reach. He struggles to climb up the pyramid of boxes built by his big brother, but once there he can't manage to keep his balance upright and has to bawl ignominiously to be helped down again.

He pays a price for all his achievements too, because every step he takes towards independence cuts him off from his mother, who so short a time ago seemed to be his other self.

In his own play-world, a child can be lord and master of the nursery or captain of his toy boat.

So all early 'play' is marked by a conflict between the wish to be himself and separate (he uses the pronouns 'I' or 'me' only when he is fully two years old), and the desire to remain close to his mother. He plays a game of offering a toy, then snatching it back, he runs away and urges her to 'catch me!', delirious when she sweeps him up in her arms and says, 'I've got you!' Holding hands, letting go—in play of this kind tiny children ward off the spectre of loneliness, the private world that is the lot of every man.

In his nursery, the child externalizes his troubles. There, at least, he is lord and master. The boy with the pig farm has the power of life and death over his animals, and can decide who is for the butcher and who for the pen. He can provide food and safety. Other children may prove unwilling, or may remind him of his true stature, and then he is likely to complain, 'Why do I always have to have someone else in to play?' Only because he has been able in these ways to satisfy his lust for power, his need to be a giant in a lilliputian world, is he able to consent to stand still while his hands and face are washed before tea—to feel actual relief at being told once again what to do.

At times, indeed, a sense of power is unbearable, choice is impossible, and splendid isolation is too much for children to endure. Then their playthings lie scattered and abandoned and they ask for nothing better than to tag round the house

after mother with duster and brush, or to fall into step beside daddy wandering down the garden, hands clasped behind back in perfect imitation. By such serious mimicry children try for comradeship with grown-ups they love, a feeling of unity hard to maintain when you are, as most children are, at the beck and call of most adults. The little boy cajoling his pigs to 'be good and eat it up', the little girl parting her hair in the middle and sucking in her cheeks to make herself look older—both are being mummy, retreating in fantasy perhaps even as far back as those blissful days before birth when mother and child were one creature.

But discoveries come hard on each other's heels, and if he is to survive in his expanding world, the child must carry on with his voyage *alone*. It is through his body that he does this—and in his earliest days, more through the senses of smell, taste and touch, which can be used to examine what is close at hand, than through sight and hearing, which probe what is distant. He learns to walk, and comes to feel, without being able to explain it, the concept of space. 'Fast' and 'slow' have meaning when he chases or is caught, 'noisy' and 'quiet' when he hides and then jumps out on a playmate, 'gently' and 'roughly' when he puffs a feather or bangs a drum. He can see his teddy bear through the garden door which is of glass, but not through the hall door because that is made of wood. The round ball rolls, but the box has corners and will not move. Teddy is furry,

like mother's dress—and that's wool. His egg has a pointed end that is easily bashed with a spoon—its roundness reminds him also of his ball. The bath water floats his duck because the duck is light, but his metal submarine won't float because it is heavy. He stands *on* a chair to be king of the castle, hides *behind* something when he wants to frighten his sister, puts his soldiers *in* a box.

These things are so taken for granted, once they have been achieved, that it is almost impossible for an adult or an older child to imagine the fantastic amount of sorting and classifying and arranging the material world into categories for easy reference, which a small child at play has to perform. At three months he may cry for the moon outside the window because he hasn't learned the facts of distance or size. At four years he will sing happily, 'The cow jumped over the moon.' At seven, he is contemptuous of such unscientific notions and will argue why something like 'The man in the moon came down too soon and asked his way to Norwich' is pure nonsense.

It is above all through play of this sort, which is basically intellectual play, that speech develops, for the child needs to ask, check, argue, plan, give orders, make decisions. His questions tumble out and he keeps up a running commentary on his actions, setting out aloud his thoughts and fancies. He states his problems aloud and solves them in the same way: 'My sand pie won't turn out—the sand's too dry—I'll damp it

a bit—there! I've put too much water in—it's gone to mud . . . That's better! Now stick a flag in the top—this'll do—no, it's too thick—it'll crack the top—this thin one is better . . .' The more he learns to use words, the more competently he is able to plan his play, as well as to organize other children in a game ('Listen, you!—you're on my side . . .').

But speech will not do everything for him. He chatters away, but there are and will always be some things he can't express adequately in words—feelings that lie too deep, things he doesn't know, or doesn't wish to know, or does not dare say. The boy with the pig farm, for example, playing so innocently—it may well be that the pigs going off to the butcher in the van represent his daddy, his brothers and sisters, and that when they have gone he will feel that he is left, as deep down he sometimes wishes to be, both the owner of the house and mummy's favourite baby, having to share her love with no one else.

In fact, much of a child's play provides him with a bridge between his feelings and the expression of those feelings in words. When he has been beaten in a game, or been hurt or frustrated, he can ease the wound by playing out his emotion. Play helps him especially with those hurts and furies that come from his limited power over language. No matter how verbally gifted a child is, or how ready his parents are to listen to him, he still needs the concrete medium of play to help him

113

in expressing abstract thought. The psychologist Margaret Lowenfeld, who set her small patients to build their miniature worlds in sand-trays, points out that in this symbolic form children drained off excess emotional energy that otherwise might have remained dammed up and so have led to disturbed and unhappy behaviour.

Of course, the understanding that children's play has therapeutic purposes like these, naturally leads adults to see in play all sorts of meanings that a child lacks the words to express. Many a psychiatrist, poring anxiously over the paintings done by the children in his care, will read into a sombre use of colour evidence of untold fears or doubts, into an array of toy wild animals symbols of suppressed aggression. Is it possible that the way a little girl deals with her dolls— whether she habitually nags or reprimands or protects them —indicates her attitude to her own mother and to her idea of motherhood? Sometimes such interpretations of simple behaviour seem (and are) unnecessarily complicated. But certainly, if we know a child well and listen carefully to what he is saying, we can discover much about his attitude to his own particular world—what people and things he finds threatening or worrying, and what solace he most needs.

Though all children normally play with much the same toys, their use of those toys is individual and is governed by particular needs that may often be hidden from grown-ups. What we can safely recognize as a general function of play is the release of emotion—emotion which cannot be given vent to in any other way and which parents may not understand until it is revealed in the changed behaviour afterwards. A toddler, banished from his mother's side because she is busy bathing baby, may run into the garden, send the cat squealing over the wall, dash his football thunderingly against the fence, take a running jump to grab a prize dahlia, pick up a stick and whang it through the air—all this and more, before coming back into the house smiling, to ask with great politeness for orange juice. His anger has been channelled, and he has proved to himself that he is a person of some account and can do terrible things. His 'purposeless' play has been of immeasurable value to him and has helped him, as we say, to 'come to his senses'.

Similarly, in play a child can rid himself of forbidden wishes and thoughts without feeling guilty or risking punishment. Making fortifications in the garden till his hands are black with mud, floating boats in the gutter, messing about with sand and water or paint and paste—these are activities usually tolerated by adults who would not allow him for a second to do the things for which they are substitutes—investigate his faeces and urine, those precious products of his body. In play, he can be dirty and destructive, he can throw and kick—and the grown-ups will smile. To some degree, too, he can use play to satisfy his curiosity about sex. Little girls stuff a pillow under a dress to simulate pregnancy, lift up a jersey to suckle a baby doll, change the doll's nappy and poke its genital region. Left together, children will play games in which they are doctors examining patients, or they will draw or model people with sexual organs, and by pretending to hide these products and giggling over them will tempt adults into explaining the mysteries involved.

Many forms of play allow children, overtly and within limits, to satisfy impulses of spite and cruelty, the magic excuse being, 'I didn't mean it—it was only in fun. . . . It was just a game. . . . We were only playing.' They will 'accidentally' trip up and knock down, they will pounce out frighteningly on a timid playmate, they will capture another child and tie him up until the victim is shedding real tears. But as often as not, such aggressive feelings find harmless outlets—in castles that are demolished, trains that crash and dolls that have to be tended in hospital.

Play does all these things, not only for disturbed children who may come to the attention of teacher or psychiatrist, but for *every* child. We all suffer feelings of despair and frustration after all. Instinctively children seek to free themselves from these feelings, which means that whenever two or three children meet together and cry, 'Let's play mothers and fathers . . .' they begin with a body of common needs, to be worked out through their game. Adults often say, 'They'll soon make friends', and the reason this expectation is usually justified lies in the shared emotional background of the children, and in the common stock-in-trade they bring to their make-believe.

Adults try to encourage the maturing process in play by providing more and more complicated toys, from the simple-shaped duck (for clutching) to elaborate metal construction sets (for building skyscrapers). But the clearest demonstration *through play* of the development of a child's personality is given when a two-year-old, at first using her doll's tea-set to give herself a drink, will later offer a drink to her mother. Later still, she will see that her dolls are provided for, seated comfortably, each with her plate and cup, and will act as hostess to them. From living in a world of which she is the centre, she has developed to the point where she includes other people and wonders what she can do for them.

The reverse is also true. Children often use play as a legitimate way of regressing. A hefty eleven-year-old, for example, may have a favourite game in which she is her little sister's baby: she will squat down to be led about, have her hair combed, be naughty, refuse to go to bed, and talk in a high-pitched babyish voice. Through this play, exasperating as it almost always is to everyone else, she may be seeking points of escape from the pressure always to be the 'big girl' of the family, always to be at the head of the class.

If play is of primary importance in a child's world, it is not, however, a panacea for childish ills or troubles, nor does it *necessarily* provide a favourable climate for the development of mental health. An aggressive child, for example, who is allowed to go wild in the belief that he must 'get it off his chest' and makes havoc of a playroom, will end worse off than he began. Again, forcing timid children into play with others because they 'must learn to mix' will only sharpen their fears and make them even less confident. More play groups, more adventure playgrounds, more playing space will not inevitably bring about a generation of relaxed, well-balanced individuals. All play may be viewed as a simple kind of therapy. But it is, of course, much much more than that, perhaps full of delights and dangers which we do not yet guess at, and may never as adults know or understand.

Patterns of play

These are very simple drawings—a making of marks on the most convenient canvas of all, the ground. The small Japanese girl draws houses, roads and a boundary with chalk, and sticks pieces of paper into the cracks in the pavement for trees. Childish as the work is, the girl takes the trouble to create a replica of a rather complex formal world.

The Pitjantjatjara aborigine children of Australia sit languid and naked—and will go naked until adolescence—in the grounds of a mission station. They are taking no pains, but turn lazily in the heat, using their hands and feet to describe circles about themselves in the dust.

Sticks and stones

In the heart of the African Transkei the name of the game is Iitonga, which to nobody's surprise means 'sticks'. But whether in Africa, or on a sidewalk in Palma where these two Majorcan boys are boldly crossing imaginary scimitars, or anywhere else in the world, the improvised armoury of childhood includes just about everything: sticks, stones, swords, staves, knives, slings and arrows, and the trusty blunderbuss found in Grandfather's closet.

Psychiatrists suggest that a fighting game is a useful way of working off natural aggressions. It is lamentably true that, therapy or not, fighting seems to be fun.

Ropes are for sliding . . .

Whatever happens to be there is the inspiration of all sorts of children's games. These girls, sliding down a rope in a Swedish garden, are doing what has come naturally to tomboys since time began. And someone, thousands of years ago, must have realized that stones are good for something else besides throwing at people. Flipping up in the air and trying to catch, for instance. The result was the game being played by Hong Kong urchins (top right) and in Algeria (below). Pictures of it exist on jars from ancient Greece and on a fresco in Pompeii, and it is still played all over the world under various names like fivestones, jacks, and knucklebones, and with nearly everything from stones, sheep bones, jacks and seeds, to cloth bags.

'round and 'round

The man who invented the wheel no doubt had the most serious intentions. He certainly set civilization and commerce ahead a great deal. But one of the most cheerful by-products of it all was the kind of fun almost anyone can have with something that rolls. History teaches us that the hoop was used in the sixteenth century in performances of acrobatics and dancing. The African boy at right, with a little help from a twist of metal and a spokeless bicycle wheel, is demonstrating a still older use however. Marbles must have begun the moment when tools first became good enough to make hard substances round enough to roll. Roller-skating is more recent, spreading across America and Europe in the late nineteenth century. It is now a favourite of children almost everywhere—including, at left, Paris.

Hop, skip and jump

With or without benefit of rope, hopping, skipping and running are games in themselves. At Chamonix two French girls are being helped at the skipping rope by their elders. The Afghanistan boys (below left) are hopping, too, but on one leg, in a game of tag. Below, at Bouake on the Ivory Coast, boys play a faster, two-footed version of the same game, zig-zagging through the dusty heat of their village.

125

'Two . . . four . . . six . . . eight . . .'

Organized sport is more than fun. It carries with it the burden of team endeavour and personal honour, the troublesome need to submerge individuality in a team effort. If team devotion and discipline often help make men of boys, team spirit has been known to make boys of men, too.

Left: Barefoot rugby in New Zealand, where the traditional British sports are pursued with even more fervour than they are in Britain.

Right: Barefoot cricket in South Africa is probably less inspired by the Old School Tie than by native energy.

Below: Although the French political scene is, temporarily at least, no longer a tug-of-war, Parisian school-boys carry on this old tradition.

The fascination of a ball . . .

. . . is to throw, to catch, to kick, and sometimes to watch.

Left: A French boy leans into a kick in Paris.

Below, left: English schoolgirls play an invented game, a cross between rugby and netball, on a grass pitch in High Wycombe.

Below: An American boy puts 'body-English' on a pitch.

Right: English prep school boys, restricted by dress and lack of space, turn football into a spectator sport.

Mind over matter

A busy hospital dealing with emergencies, a canoe in tricky water, the heroic passing of the bull before the kill—these are really moments in the mind. But the rich play of the imagination needs a few makeshift props.

The 'hospital' is at a school in Bethnal Green, London, where children are encouraged to copy adult activities with carefully supplied equipment. The 'canoe' is a stretch of bank in Arnhem Land, Australia, where aboriginal children, too young to pilot canoes like their fathers, nevertheless have got hold of real paddles. The 'bull' being used by these two boys in Madrid is a home-made contraption with wooden handles. But it has real horns.

Sudden playground in the snow

Snow lifts up the heart of any child in the early morning and makes breakfast a thing to be impatiently rushed. Then out in coats and woolly caps and boots that crunch and sloosh in the new whiteness. There is the trek up the hill and the gliding swoop downwards, and wet mittens and the struggle to stand up. There is the breath that you can see, and the beating of hands and stamping of feet, and the sharp cry of voices especially clear. Back at home, there are hot drinks and towels and a great warmth spreading in the mind and blood, and the earnest hope that it will happen again tomorrow.

Shots fired in imitation

A gun for most boys is a wonderful and compulsive thing. It is a subtle toy, a symbol of potency, a key to the roles of defender, hero, agressor.

The war-game in London's Mayfair seems slightly more frightening than the French Davy Crockett . . . perhaps because Davy Crockett is now a distant and romantic figure, while war is served up every day in the headlines. But for the young, the taking of Berlin and the fall of the Alamo belong to equally high and far-off times.

One of the blessings of the world of children is that nobody has to teach a small boy and his big brother how to dig in the sand or hurl rocks in the sea. Grown-ups, however, sometimes forget the secret.

Exploration

'The child would know all the properties of things, their innermost nature. For this reason he examines the object on all sides; for this reason he breaks it; for this reason he puts it in his mouth and bites it. We reprove the child for his naughtiness and foolishness; and yet he is wiser than we who reprove him.'

—Friedrich Froebel

Besides true scientists, children are about the only people in the world who still reach out towards the unknown. The great ages of global exploration are past, and space exploration may go on forever. The realization that man can never know everything has taken the excitement out of discovery. But children continue to look for answers, because they really believe they are going to find them. Like the scientist, they have an inborn faith in the ultimate rationality of the universe.

Everyone has made these first discoveries—of the sea-sound in a shell, insects in the grass, reflections in the mirror. But first explorations, instead of being consciously remembered, are absorbed into the personality and become inseparable from it. 'Children ought to begin writing their autobiographies in the cradle.' This suggestion is put forward in the following chapter by Anthony Thwaite, editor and poet. He vividly describes the impact of life on the demanding exploratory mind of a child, reminding us that there is a great deal of fun as well as science in these first explorations. Gibberish, for instance, is the exploration of language, but it is also the mother-tongue of childhood, complete with its own poetry.

The picture essay is an illustration of all aspects of exploration, from scouting lizards in Australia (p. 148) to sneaking a first smoke in the Mato Grosso (p. 163).

The world in a grain of sand

Anthony Thwaite

'Issues from the hand of God, the simple soul'
To a flat world of changing lights and noise,
To light, dark, dry or damp, chilly or warm;
Moving between the legs of tables and of chairs,
Rising or falling, grasping at kisses and toys,
Advancing boldly, sudden to take alarm,
Retreating to the corner of arm and knee,
Eager to be reassured. . . .

from *Animula*, by T. S. Eliot

The process begins in one room, and in one particular part of one room, and moves out from there. At first there is restriction and constriction: swaddling clothes, perhaps, and an immobility in the face of noise, light, darkness, faces. There is only a voice—that is all you have, it is your own:

A baby crying in the night
And with no language but a cry.

But what makes the voice, the cry, is hunger, pain, fear. At first happiness makes silence and silence happiness. There is no exploration. The cradle, the carri-cot, the apple-box, the bottom-drawer, arms that pick up and hold tight.

Then the baby begins to discover its own body, clasping and unclasping its hands like a sad old woman. A ball of shot silk twirls its colours round and round above the cot, and gradually the eyes begin to focus and to follow it. The fixed, almost blind, stare turns to recognition, to curiosity. One day someone puts an absurd plastic doll, light as air and with an inane little bell inside it, on to the blankets by the sleeping body—and suddenly there's a jingling from the cot, and there Alice lies, banging the doll with aimless little paws and looking puzzled at the result.

The baby, immobile in its pram, is exposed to an alarming world of huge, seamy, pocked, smelly, grimacing, well-meaning, unknown faces, peering in and floating like uncertain moons an inch or two away. These first intrusions open up a terrifying area of uncertainty. Leave a baby in its pram outside a shop and then come back a few minutes later: the chances are that someone will be bent double over the tiny supine figure, chattering and gurgling in the friendliest possible way, but quite without any idea how strange, even grotesque, that animated white disc must seem to the trapped creature underneath. At this stage, the child carries his world round with him, shifted in his pram or in someone's arms, but still a transportable lump at the mercy of anyone who swims into his ken. What must he think, lying there transfixed, without bearings and without any sense of direction?

Now, movement and exploration depend on how much freedom you get. A Japanese child for a long time is swaddled, contained: held to its mother's back, strapped at seat and back, it lolls asleep, kept asleep by natural movements as the mother goes about her business, or jogged playfully up and down when she's standing still. The world is a close place, a padded back and the smell of black glossy hair, drenched in camellia oil.

With freedom, limbs and muscles begin to assert themselves. Kicking, flinging out arms; beginning to sit up, at first tremulously uncertain, then with firm, deliberate confidence, then ease; on hands and knees, beginning to crawl, sometimes solidly and four-square, sometimes with a crablike sideways shuffle, or with one leg trailing uselessly. One hand steadies the stance, the other darts out like a lizard's tongue to grasp toy, food, coal, the dog. The room is circumnavigated, harried, conquered.

But this is still one room. Outside there is a garden, a field, a street, sky. There's the moon, which (according to his father in *The Nightingale*) pacified little Hartley Coleridge like others before and since. The baby lies on his back in the play-pen and watches birds as he watched his silk ball; and now he sits and reaches for them, swooping and fluttering. The press of sensations must be so hectic, so various, that it's a wonder all babies don't suffer from pronounced hyperaesthesia. Perhaps they do. But they can't tell us.

They can tell us they don't like this cereal, that curious sloshy mess of a Junior Dinner. With a smart eyes right the head turns and the parent's proffered spoon jabs into thin air; or out goes the splayed hand and down on the floor goes the spoon, cereal and all. All this is brute and random action, without words.

Words are the beginning of a new kind of exploration. But before the right definable and defined words arrive, there are torrents of gibberish to wade through, sounds approximating to words, sounds which—through repetition—parents begin to interpret correctly. How colossal that step forward, through millions of years of trial and preparation, when 'Mama' and 'Dada' first break through the babble of incoherent noise! Lips that seem to have no purpose but eating and sucking and blowing and gurgling, lips that move like some as yet unperfected plastic, take on a firmness and definition as they shape their first words, exploring the foothills of semantics.

To name is in some measure to understand, to cope with what happens. When my eldest daughter was two she saw the snow for the first time, but she knew *about* it already: she had already heard the word. Later, I wrote this:

'White snow', my daughter says, and sees
For the first time the lawn, the trees,
Loaded with this superfluous stuff.
Two words suffice to make facts sure
To her, whose mental furniture
Needs only words to say enough.

Perhaps by next year she'll forget
What she today saw delicate
On every blade of grass and stone;
Yet will she recognize those two
Syllables, and see them through
Eyes which remain when snow has gone?

Season by season, she will learn
The names when seeds sprout, leaves turn,
And every change is commonplace.
She will bear snowfalls in the mind,
Know wretchedness of rain and wind,
With the same eyes in a different face.

A one-year-old girl sets out on her first expedition into the gentle jungle of an English summer.

There is nothing more surprising than the discovery of one's own image in the dressing-table mirror—unless it is the discovery that mother's cosmetics can radically alter that image.

My wish for her, who held by me
Looks out now on this mystery
Which she has solved with words of mine,
Is that she may learn to know
That in her words for the white snow
Change and permanence combine—
The snow melted, the trees green,
Sure words for hurts not suffered yet, nor seen.

The new words, as they come, have mostly to do with will and appetite: 'Me want . . .', and what is wanted is chocolate biscuit, doll, crayon, drink, pot, that cat, that boy's biscuit, that girl's doll, someone else's drink, *my* pot; perhaps a hug. There isn't much room for abstractions. For a long time the world of things is enough to keep the vocabulary expanding and growing, grasping the seen, the desirable, rejecting the disliked, the feared.

A kind of discrimination begins in the way in which things are explored. At first there's a cursoriness which shows itself in the restless moving on from object to object: mobility is the important thing, not inspection. But then some particular toy, perhaps, holds the child for an hour, as its parts and recesses and possibilities are fingered and experimented with. Some adults affect to despise so-called 'educational' toys, and indeed it's an unfortunate term, for any toy worth having teaches a child something about noticing and controlling the world. Those hours spent in screwing and unscrewing wooden nuts and bolts are hours spent in acquiring not just manual dexterity but self-confidence too. And the clockwork animal that runs gibbering up and down the floor half a dozen

times and then can't be made to work any more—that teaches something as well, though it teaches something the manufacturers never intended.

The adult urban world of words, jobs, equipment, is for a long time too difficult for the child to take in. In the country it's easier. A country child can begin to grasp the idea of his father's work quite quickly, and all over the world small children feed the pigs, scare off the rooks, glean the cornfields, learn the names of the cows, and take the sheep out on the hills. These seem natural explorations, and the progress from child to man not only natural but accelerated. In Libya I've seen boys of six or seven leading a camel as it walks sullenly back and forth at the wells that irrigate the fields, and in Sardinia a boy of the same age out on the hillside with his father's goats. These are the responsibilities of work in cultures which have no time to let their children explore gradually through play: these boys are miniature adults, and as such they have to learn quickly. But when they play, they play in the same world as the urban child, with the same drives and appetites.

Rehearsing for adulthood is a full-time occupation. 'Mothers and fathers' is a figuring-out, a miming, of whatever seems graspable and imitable in the puzzling observed lives of their parents and their friends' parents: the long hours spent arranging bedding for dolls, portioning out mock food, tending sick dolls and younger siblings—these are the gropings towards becoming what they inevitably will become. School, when it comes, is not simply a new way of spending the day, or of adjusting to the social world, or a formal mode in which things are learned, but an extension, again, of the imitable

142

world. No sooner are they back from school in the afternoon than they begin arranging desks, chairs, and blackboard in their own rehearsal, their own re-living, of the experiences they have just gone through. The imposed adult world is not enough—they need to re-create it for themselves, often unconsciously underlining its oddity with their own interpretation: listen, for example, to the way in which a child catches the too sweet modulations in the headmistress's speech, breathily stressing all those genteel mannerisms, and all completely without any notion of satire or, indeed, of comment. Another mask has been put on, another set of gestures absorbed, to be part of the whole complex equipment of personality.

The body, too, is a strange new piece of equipment to be explored, usually as matter-of-factly as anything else. Whatever Freud and Melanie Klein have unwrapped of a child's sexual drives, plain observation seems to show that a young child's sexuality manifests itself no more and no less than half a dozen other characteristics.

It's a deeply sensuous world, certainly, of touching and tasting and smelling: 'the licking and rushing' W. H. Auden writes about. As the world begins to expand, so do the appetites and the capacity, too, for letting the fancy play with them:

'I like paper too. If you gave me a piece of paper and I didn't want to draw a picture I'd eat it.'
'I'm so hot I'd like to sleep on a frozen pond.'

Some children are demonstrative in their affections, some not: the affectionate child is open about the pleasures of

hugging and being hugged, kissing and being kissed. But no child rejects comfort, even if it is only the comfort of some inanimate thing which must be sniffed or plucked or sucked before going to sleep—the adored and fondled talisman, which may be a shred of blanket, a ribbon, a ball of fluff, a glove, an otherwise loathsome woollen animal, or—animate but distinct—his own thumb. Sleep is such a strange thing, not always desirable, sometimes not easy to reach, so that it must be explored stealthily, with the furtive movements of the sniffer, plucker, or sucker.

In sleep, dreams. For years, between the ages of about three and ten, I used to wake up screaming from a dream of a little scotty dog that came running out from under the bed. I never knew why it was so frightening, and I still don't know. But there are other night fears that are more explicable: think of Robert Louis Stevenson:

The shadows of the balusters, the shadow of the lamp,
The shadow of the child that goes to bed—
And the wicked shadows coming, tramp, tramp, tramp,
With the black night overhead.

Emily, who is seven, doesn't want to see that picture in the book of Bible stories about the wisdom of Solomon, or hear about Herod's slaughter of the Innocents: 'No, no, I'll dream about it.' Yet she wants to see the picture and read the story, too. She's in training for the more sophisticated adult delight in what horrifies and haunts. She has begun to dabble in her emotions, like any connoisseur of Dracula and the Chamber of Horrors. In a more primitive society we too would believe in the existence of her horrors; but we think we know where

the difference lies between fact and fantasy, between stories and 'the real'.

Stories and people and sensations: they stand round like presences.

His father told him that story: his father looked at him through a glass: he had a hairy face. . . . When you wet the bed first it is warm then it gets cold. His mother put on the oilsheet. That had the queer smell.

Joyce with his epiphany of the first gropings, Proust invoking childhood memories from the taste of a petit madeleine cake, the three-year-old who suddenly says excitedly 'I can kiss with my mouth!'—all of them explore the same sensuous world, from different ends of 'the telescope of time'. In autumn, for children out in the garden picking apples, two things are at work: the following of adult directions as apples are graded into undamaged eaters off the tree, cookers, damaged windfalls worth eating, rotten ones for the compost, and so on; and the sense, in grading them, that even these taken-for-granted fruits of the earth have an individuality, a peculiarity, which they'd never noticed before. 'Look how this one squashes! And this one has a wasp in it! And this one is split right down the middle! And I'm eating this one and it's lovely!'

'I can kiss with my mouth and I can eat with it too.'

But the frustrations too. Hours spent trying to make things: a puppet theatre out of bits of coloured paper glued together —it won't stand up but flops about all over the place, and the parts come unstuck, and the fingers are jammed stickily together, and it all ends in tears. Or learning, simply, that a tricycle two feet wide won't go between a wall and a table one foot apart. Or trying to paint when the paint is too wet and the paper too absorbent and the brush begins to take lumps out of the paper. Most kinds of adult comfort are no good on these occasions. What's wrong is nothing that can be put right by saying 'I know it's very difficult' or 'Never mind, try again another time' or—most irritating—'I think you've done very well'. What's wrong is the raw feeling of personal inadequacy, that here's an intractable world not to be tamed. Certain things are—fair enough—an adult prerogative, and you go to a grown-up to have something done: a needle threaded, a difficult doll's head put back on, a hem mended. But the acts that come out of a child's own head are for him alone while he wrestles with them, and the tears are the tears of the *poète manqué*: 'I made it and it won't stay together!'

There is always so much to learn, and no one knows what will be held forever in some little fold or cul-de-sac of the brain and what will be lost as if it had never been. Years ago, when Emily was so young that it sometimes seems there was nothing for her to remember but that *we* have to carry it all round in our heads so that we can supply her with an extreme childhood, some soot fell down the chimney on a particularly windy night: not a lot of it, really, but enough to slop about the carpet a bit beyond the fireplace. That soot is clear and vivid in her mind, and is always being fetched out as an illustration of something or nothing. Why that soot? Why not the aeroplane that took us to Germany, or the woman whom she saw fall down on the pavement with a heart-attack, or, come

to that, the first time she saw snow and could use the right words? Some bits of the jigsaw of experience, some fragments of exploration, are absorbed so completely that they simply become part of gesture, thought, being. What will remain distinct, as a specific memory, is unpredictable. Children ought to begin writing their autobiographies in the cradle. In some ways perhaps they do.

A lot of things have to be explored together, with others who have reached the same stage, the same set of skills. In those episodic plays constructed in the shadow of visits to the pantomime or *Peter Pan* or *Let's Make an Opera* action is limited and most of it goes on in the head. Words take on the cadences of refrains. 'He's dead. Ah, he's dead, he's de-a-d!' Each actor is involved in a common ritual, yet separate. 'Now I'll be the witch and I'll come out of my cave—this is my cave—and you—you're the little girl now—run away from me, and then I'll come running after you, and you have to drop dead when I say. And then a fairy comes along—you be the fairy, Caroline—and then . . .' 'No, I'll be a good wolf and I'll bite the witch and . . .' So they improvise, spontaneously bringing into action all their accumulated half-knowledge, scraps of stories and plays, making together—with give and take—a performance which has never been written and is never to be repeated.

Such exploration needs freedom, an openness of experience which isn't all the time hedged about with prohibitions and taboos. Children at this stage are quick to sense adult disapproval, scorn, or boredom, and are not eager to have adults 'co-operating', except in the rare situations where adults can take part on completely equal terms. Such a situation comes about—sometimes—when the child becomes a fervent collector.

Most children collect, and most collect without order or strategy; and why not? They aren't, after all, museums spending public money. They probably aren't spending at all. Dr J. A. Hadfield quotes the itemized contents of one boy's pockets, and there is no common factor in those contents: they are simply accumulations. I think of the museum I put together between the ages of seven and ten, and it was like a parody of Elias Ashmole's 'cabinet of curiosities'. There was a stone from Bolton Castle and a stone from Fountains Abbey, a grass-snake's skin, a German soldier's cap, fossils, butterflies, Roman coins, a stuffed swordfish, stamps, a Victorian snuff-box with a loose lid, a monocle, some jars of vile mixed liquids which contained my attempts at making poison gas, some ordinary spent cartridges, a rabbit's paw, birds' eggs, and a bit of barrage balloon. These were the palpable tokens of all my succeeding interest in history and natural history. Through these hoardings of trash and curiosities, we come to the delighted discovery that

World is crazier and more of it than we think,
Incorrigibly plural.

Behind every geologist, archaeologist, naturalist, is this caddis-worm of a child; and behind those hard-bitten or prosperous faces in Sotheby's sale-room too. The urge to discover is also the urge to possess; the exploration of knowledge is a way of coveting and grasping the known thing.

Children learn by imitating and doing, rarely by taking thought and saying, 'I shall now learn the six times table' or 'I want to know how to make a dog-kennel'. They explore their own potentiality, their own inadequacy, through random questions (and often random answers, too) and through making random shots. Gradually the alarming and unaccountable world reveals itself, sometimes in the way in which things overheard rumble away in the back of the mind and then, suddenly, fall into place and are made plain. I remember puzzling away for years at what people meant by 'digs' ('So-and-So's moving to London, and he's found digs in Clapham while they house-hunt'), never thinking to ask, and then at last quickly grasping the obvious and mundane meaning. Not only the meanings of words, but the untidy acquisition of new concepts: that milkmen are fathers too, and have holidays; that the hollow-eyed, huge-bellied child on the Oxfam poster is a real child and that children, somewhere, really do starve; that neither teachers nor parents know everything, and that even encyclopedias can be wrong; that even best friends can be hateful, and the spotty, smelly, fat boy can be nice. And reading books begins to be not only a skill but a way of exploring unimaginable as well as imaginable things: fictions often prepare the way for facts. Those cannons solemnly fired off, for example, in one of the *Babar the Elephant* books took on a firm and 'real' meaning when Lucy, aged three, saw the cannon firing their salutes at Churchill's funeral: the story was a preparation for the otherwise scarcely understandable ritual, and both were given a firmness and concreteness.

Some time around ten or eleven there's a period, often, of great secretiveness, when a lot of exploration goes on which is more like adult exploration—of strange and new country—than anything that has gone before or will happen afterwards. When I was eleven years old and lived in a part of Virginia that seemed to me like the depths of the country but which in fact was no more than the extreme outer suburbs of Washington, I spent day after summer day tracking down streams where watersnakes hung in the bushes by the bank, watching swallowtail butterflies dart and alight in the undergrowth, finding huge hollow rocks I believed were Indian grindstones, searching the ditches near the old hospital for Civil War musket-balls and cannon-balls. All this I did by myself, not because I was a particularly self-sufficient child but because I needed to find these things for myself, to know them by myself.

Or so I rationalize it now, at a distance fogged with vague memories of *Bevis*, Richard Jefferies's paean of boyhood. Fogged with *Stalky and Co.* too: not a book I ever got on with, because just as Jefferies seems to cover all that intense secret exploration with a light idyllic wash, so Kipling seems to invest all the gang-cohesion and gang-warfare of those boys with an arch and nudging scoutmasterishness. Boys at their pre-initiation practices are not there to be watched in the shrubbery by some elderly note-taker. 'Old men ought to be explorers', and so they may be; but the intense, accelerated, radical exploration was over and done with by the time they were thirteen. After that we learn things, get better at doing them, get wisdom, perhaps, or anyhow make our adjustments. But the explorer has been left behind in the jungle.

'Is it so small a thing
To have enjoyed the sun,
To have lived light in the spring . . . ?'
—Matthew Arnold

Scramble, tumble, leap and run.
Aboriginal children, naked or in
shorts, swarm over the hot rocks
looking for tasty lizards near
Ernabella Mission Station, South
Australia.

The first green leaves of April send a New York girl racing under the trees in Central Park. She has been cooped up in a skyscraper apartment all winter—so long that the feel of the spring sun seems brand new.

The discovery of something, nothing and anything

These children, all under three years old, are preoccupied with the investigation of commonplace objects. A girl in Perry County, Kentucky, sits in cut-down farmland behind her home, examining a leather pouch. The two London children (opposite and far right) find their interests running to bottles. The girl takes time out from a shopping trip with her mother in order to examine a crate of empty milk bottles; the boy, testing his mechanical genius, will soon make at least one real discovery— corkscrews don't work on plastic tops.

Things want looking into

London: The brass, snake-headed
horn on a vintage car.

Tokyo: A display book in a stationery store.

New York: A raft level view of a lens and shutter.

How to get to the top

A girl in north London rings the bell
—the hard way.

A Greek boy in Rhodes scales a
fountain.

A boy in southern England enjoys life at the top of a concrete lamp post.

An Indian tot in Calcutta struggles up the decorative mosaic steps of the Jain temple, with hardly any help from her big brother's tennis shoes.

There it was, all his, a real car

South coast rubbish dump, England. Enter Gordon, a fair, curious, bespectacled boy. Suddenly, magic in the shape of a motor car, alone, unattended, mysterious, an abandoned symbol of the adult world. Gordon moves centre-stage, fingers, pokes, pries. Nobody says 'no'. The car gives no tremor. Gordon looks (why not?) into the works; climbs (why not?) into the driving-seat; takes the wheel. It doesn't matter that the body has no bonnet, the headlamps no bulbs. For an hour it's all his, the best drive he ever drove.

Getting around

These boys approach Oxford Street, London's busiest, with an air of unruffled boredom. No fear and trembling for them for they've brought along a marvellous gun that fires table-tennis balls—just in case.

Managing the tricky wooden steps off the pier at Blackpool, England.

Managing, with authority, push-to-cross street lights at a busy intersection in Paris.

Creek in North America.

River in southern England.

Garden in Johannesburg.

Water's a bit of all right

To drink from, paddle in, swim in,
see your reflection in, catch small
fish in, even, if absolutely necessary,
to wash in—water is the very thing,
even when it is gurgling at the
bottom of a drain that captures
careless marbles.

Drain in the East End of London.

Acquiring a taste for the tawny weed

Everybody knows that men read
newspapers and smoke cigarettes.
And every boy wants to be a man.

In Kentish Town, London, two boys
experiment with a cigarette end
found in the street.

In Cuzco, Peru, a non-subscriber
scans the sports page.

In Brazil, a long-haired boy of the
Caraya tribe in the Mato Grosso
conducts absorbing experiments
with tobacco in the privacy of the
thick jungle forest.

Following page: On a winter day
three intrepid British girls and one
reluctant pup explore the heights
above the cliffs of Dover.

163

Practising feminine arts

A four-year-old's attempt to dress up for a party is a smashing success. The dress looks better back-to-front anyway.

Californians, wearing their own hand-painted creations, prepare to exhibit their devotion to the Beatles.

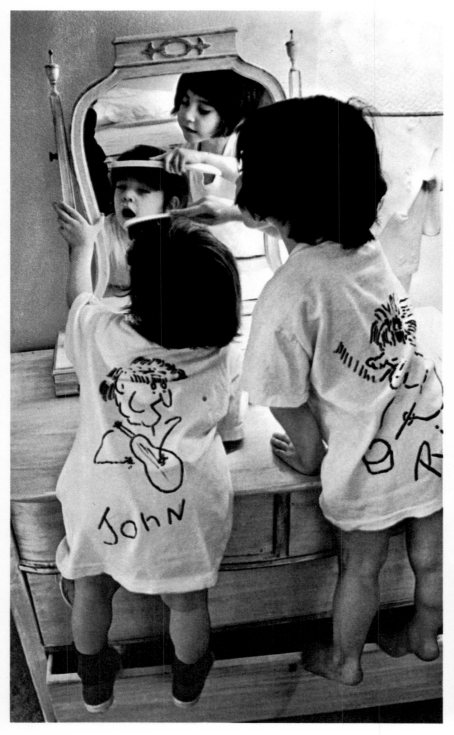

Wearing her first long formal, a
bridesmaid at a wedding reception
in London vanishes her elegant
surroundings with a wave of her
new fur muff.

Climbing a tree is, to a boy, a basic
urge, a need, a positive compulsion.
Part of the fascination is the danger
—something he won't really
understand until he hangs, terrified,
from a swaying branch.

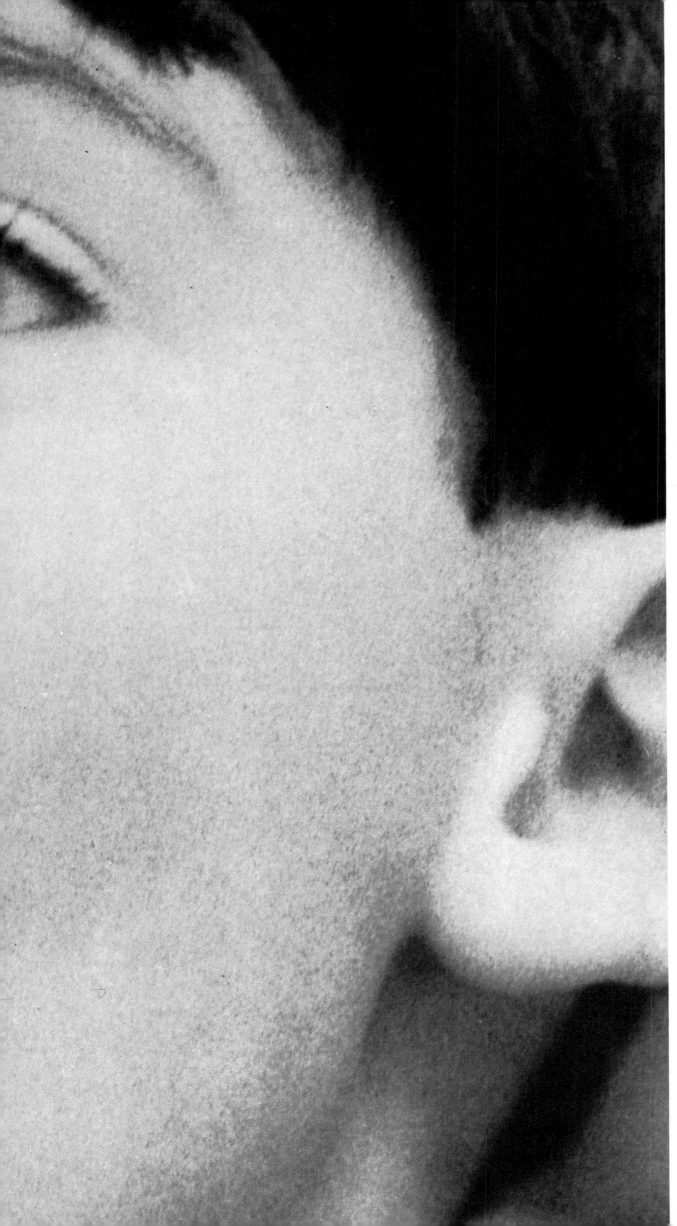

Fear and Wonder

'The one universal element in consciousness which is fundamental to life is wonder . . .'
—D. H. Lawrence

Wonder is very highly valued by adult society. All the best things are called 'wonderful'. Grown-ups often wish to look at a painting or read a poem with the uncomplicated reactions of a wondering child. But the kind of wonder and delight which shows in the face of the boy at left is only one aspect of the awe which is natural to children. The other is fear.

We are all born with certain innate fears. The grasping reflex, which exists even before birth, is the primitive reaction to the uneasy feeling of falling. Newborn babies react to sudden loud noises, as well. Both of these basic 'fears' are instinctive reflexes to sudden things that upset the nervous equilibrium.

Fear is the instinctive first reaction to things that are inexplicably unpleasant, just as wonder is the instinctive first reaction to things that are inexplicably pleasant. Both are characteristically child-like, because both, basically, are reactions to the unknown. Adults cannot return to innocence except, briefly and vicariously, by watching children. 'As we comfort their fears, they reward us with delight,' writes Alastair Reid in the following essay. 'In exchange for the promise of a future, they give us back an awareness of the present.' Author of five children's books, poet Reid is well qualified to help adults look at the world through the eyes of children.

Within the picture essay that completes this chapter, children's reactions to such worldly things as dogs, policemen, anacondas and Santa Clauses may delight and surprise even a most sophisticated reader.

'Men fear death, as children fear the dark'

Alastair Reid

Any talk about childhood is invention, since it comes from people who are no longer children. That they *were* children once is true; but by now they have trimmed their memories so suitably to recreate a useful and acceptable version of their early selves that all their talk of childhood would be totally unacceptable, even if comprehensible, to the children they once were.

Children know nothing about childhood, and have little to say about it. They are too busy becoming something they have not quite grasped yet, something which keeps changing, to be able to tell what it is. Nor will they realize what is happening to them until they are too far beyond it to remember how it felt.

The notion of childhood is, therefore, a paradox, in that childhood exists only as afterthought. As for our own children, we look at them as though, having qualified through our own childhood, we know everything about them—until suddenly, they astound us out of ourselves, and give us a glimpse of the vast distances between us and them, between the selves we are and the selves we have left far behind. I always see, as the image of this paradox, a child and a man looking at one another, warily, the one confronting what he does not know yet, the other mystified by what he can no longer remember.

And so, there are two quite distinct things—to write about childhood, or one's own childhood (or children, and one's own children); and to be a child. It is possible to remember a happening, and even to watch it happen again to a child, from the distance of our present, but to feel the puzzlement of its happening, as it once happened to us, is beyond us now, though not beyond our sympathies. Now, besides being afraid, we have an idea what fear is, whereas children are afraid long before the idea of fear can ever occur to them. In the same way, as children, we wondered at almost everything; and now, as grown-ups, we can only wonder where that wonder went.

'Did you have a happy childhood?' is a false question. As a child, I did not know what being happy was and, whether I was happy or not, I was too busy *being* to realize it. Nor did I have any idea when my childhood had begun or would end. I suppose that the question, translated, means 'Have you (as you presently are) decided to regard your childhood as a happy one?' or 'Have you decided to retain, from your childhood, the bright images, or the dark ones?' The question 'Are you happy?', put to a child, so obviously demands the answer 'yes' that it insults children by misunderstanding their nature.

Fear and wonder, or, rather, being afraid and wondering, are, for a child, so close together, so much the same impulse, that at times they are one and the same thing. Pressed too far, wonder turns into fear, as the tooth, pressed, turns pleasure to pain. 'Awe' is the word that perhaps serves best, for it embraces both fear and wonder at once.

To return to the image of the man and child staring at one another, I find the distance between them almost insuperable. The difficulties on each side are almost equally insurmountable—that of the man to persuade the child that its fears are unfounded, that of the child to communicate to the man how it feels to be new in the world. So, the man looks wistfully at the child, aware of how far he has come from his first, small founderings; and the child clings incommunicably to the man, to be comforted in its fear.

Not long ago, I stepped down with my small son from a train, early on a winter morning, on to a railway platform in Scotland, deserted except for my father, who waited for us. As the train rumbled off, we stood, all three, in the whirl of steam, for a moment that seemed to me to be endless. I found myself both child and man at once, existing, as it were, in a double dimension, able to look forward and back in the same moment, to my father in his fatherhood, to my child in his childhood. And yet what principally dawned on me was the fact that we are all immutably fixed in time at such set distances from one another that it is a wonder we are able to reach across them at all. We did, however, as the steam dispersed; and we do.

In Scotland, wandering about in my haunted past, I kept coming on my various discarded selves, running into them round familiar street corners, seeing them suddenly disappear behind a hedge. I felt that they were watching me, bewildered by what I had become. I was looking for them, desperate with questions. There was a great deal we could have said to one another, all of us; but, of course, we were never able to meet. When I would trail back in the musky evenings from these days of pure epiphany, in time to catch my son on his way to bed, it was I who, when he asked me what I had been doing, found myself saying 'Oh, nothing, really.'

Incontrovertibly, the Wordsworthian notion of growing up has clung like a moss to much of our thinking on the process—the idea of small angelic creatures trailing clouds of glory, and gradually losing their auras in the grubby, dulling business of becoming boys and men. It is a kindness to call this notion romantic; more than that, it seems to be hopelessly misguided, and therefore misguiding. Similarly, the old gentlemen who speak of the 'best years of their lives' must have receded considerably from the mainstream of existence to wish themselves back into a small and puzzled frame.

Another basis for the misunderstandings and confusions with which we obscure the actualities of childhood is the tendency to look on life, not as a moving platform, but as a series of stages—childhood, adolescence, manhood, early, middle and late middle or old age. This escalation is the reason for the infuriating advice that is constantly being handed down, or, even up, by people stuck at some point on the ladder. 'Ah, but it is only a phase. When you get to be *my* age. . . .' Only children are immune to this kind of advice, for they find it unimaginable to be older than they are. It is this same thinking that breeds all the romantic reaching for

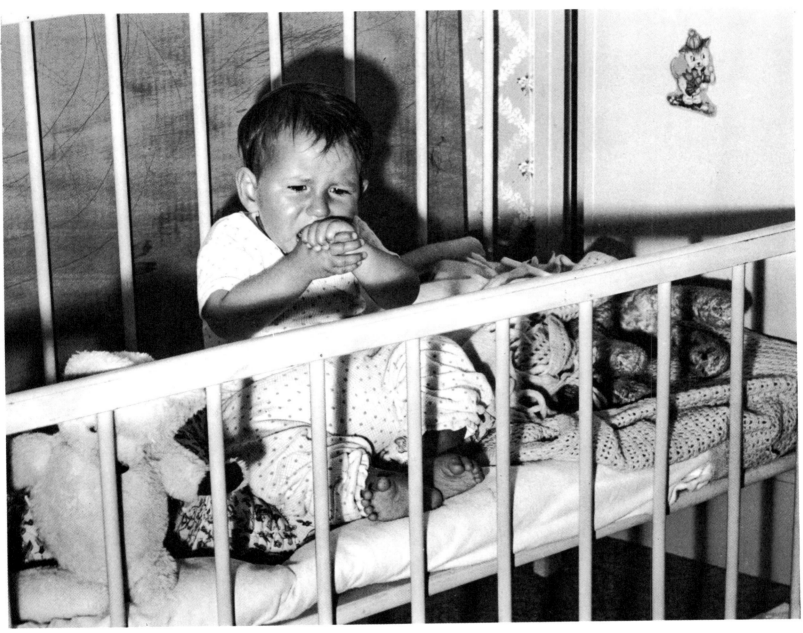

youth on the part of the middle-aged. Behind it, there is desperate regret, the regret at having missed something, of having let too much slip past unnoticed, of having lost irretrievably the most life-giving of all our impulses—the impulse of curiosity.

Children encounter three worlds—of things, people, language —all at once. First, they run slap into the physical world, the world of objects, houses, weather, gardens, machines, a profusion that seems to them inexhaustible. Simultaneously, they encounter the world of other people, of children like, but not like, themselves, of adults beyond their comprehension but within their horizon. To children, everyone else in the world is a question, and their whole lives a struggle to find a momentary answer. Gradually, however, a dialogue develops, and it dawns on them that the world is not exclusively their own. Simultaneously, too, comes the encounter with lan-

guage, for them something at first like a secret code, a way of storing their discoveries in the small islands that are their dawning minds.

The child lives in a world of particulars, so that all its feelings arise from tangible happenings. So, what truly remains in the mind from childhood is a series of very sharp images. I recall, once upon a time, at the barber's, while being shown the back of my small head in a mirror, my first glimpse, in the mirror opposite, down a long and greenish corridor, of infinity; and with that image, I recall the physical terror of the moment, which still is far more vivid to me now than any profound contemplation of the infinite.

Of course children are afraid, since the root of all fear is to be suddenly confronted with an unknown; and, to children, most of the world, on all its levels, is unknown. For them,

173

growing is a process of becoming familiar with more and more, of gradually mastering their own bafflement, of constructing, of accumulating, an identity for themselves, gradually replacing fear with confidence.

What are children afraid of? Obvious things, vast entities like the dark, thunder and lightning, incalculable animals, violence, loudness, the sea. But, besides that, an infinity of subtle things—the twisted root of a tree, a sudden shadow, an inexplicable picture. Even subtler, an expectation unsatisfied, disorientation, a disruption in the continuum of their lives. They are suddenly thrown back on themselves, only to discover that they have no self as yet. It is not simply that they are lost; much more, it is that they have no idea how to go about being found.

Fear of the dark. In a sense, it never leaves us. Obviously, in the dark, we are cut off from appearances, and driven back into our own heads, into imaginings, fantasies, dreams and nightmares. To turn on a light is at once to reveal and make contact with objects outside ourselves, and so to be distracted from our self-preoccupations. In the case of children, light convinces them that something is *there*, after all. Mornings delight them. The world has come back, as a mysterious reassurance.

As a child, I remember terrifying myself from time to time by saying, in the dark, my own name, over and over again, in a whisper. If I remember clearly, the terror arose from a sudden feeling that my name had nothing to do with me, could not explain me, existed outside of me and apart from me, and that whatever identity it gave me, there was still, separate from it, a secret self that was nameless, unknown and altogether lost.

To children, death is not really within the range of their fear, since they are incapable of having any sense of their own dying. In their world, the death of someone they have known is no more than a perplexity. What worries them is how they should act, what they should say, how they should behave. They play at being dead, in the context of a game, but it is something they always do with great enthusiasm. The absent never claims their attention as the present does.

From the vantage point of children, parents or other adults are remote, enormous, inexplicable enough to make them inevitably afraid of adult displeasure, afraid of punishment, afraid of being left alone. These fears are sufficient to make children obey beyond their understanding. But they are not, however, sufficient to make them understand. I broke the set of rules provided for me hundreds of times; and yet, I do not recall ever being afraid of the consequences, possibly because they were known, only too well known, to me. Faced with punishment, I was only impatient to have it happen to me and then to recede as quickly as possible. I doubt that fear of punishment kept me from doing anything; although it did teach me secrecy and concealment, and the humiliation of being found out.

The resilience of children. They go from tears to laughter in a matter of moments, from fear to joy unaccountably quickly. It is not simply that they have a greater capacity for forgetting than we have, or that they have less to remember. It is only that, in their constant present, each moment is obliterated by the next. Fears can recur, but can be very quickly dissipated by their being comforted or distracted. For them, while fear is momentary, wonder is endless. In the state of wonder, there is no time.

I think I ran away from home at least twice when I was a child, but obviously, I was making a gesture rather than a decision. I remember one of these occasions quite vividly. I had planned it for some days with my sister, and we had accumulated provisions, prospects and a dazzling future. As we wandered out into the day, all our earthly belongings bound up in red handkerchiefs, we moved in an ecstasy of freedom, without any trace of fear, until night began to fall. As the shadows from the hedges grew longer across the road, and as the air began to grow both darker and colder, we, in our turn, began to think again; and what we thought of was not the confusion we had run away from, but instead, positive things, like fires and lamplight, toys and hot food. We found our way back, of course, in the gathering dark; but what we never forgave our parents for was the fact that they, in their wisdom, took us back without a word, fed us, put us to bed as though nothing had happened. Our fears disappeared into rage; but we stayed at home to fight it out.

Not long ago, I watched fear happen—in this case, to my son, as we were walking down a long avenue in Spain together. Thinking that he saw me, I turned aside to buy a newspaper. I happened to glance back and in that instant, I watched him (since he had not noticed my going) turn suddenly, expecting my presence, to find me gone. He looked around, first slowly, then desperately; I could see fear start in his face, build up, and turn the placidity of the moment into sudden nightmare. 'What would you have done if I hadn't come back?' I asked him. 'I don't know,' he said. That was the fear.

On occasions, our fear *for* children far exceeds any fears they have themselves. Our imagination sees many more possibilities, and, therefore, many more dangers, than they could ever imagine.

He teeters along the crumbling top
of the garden wall, and calls 'Look up,
Papa, look up! I'm flying, I'm . . .' till
in a sudden foreseen spasm, I see him fall.
Oh, terrible
when fears lie to the senses, when the whirl
of the possible plays on the real, and plays
havoc with this
still happening. Falling. Falling
is a fright in me. Too late, too soon, I call
'Watch, watch!' and move in time to catch
his small sweat-beaded body, still enchanted

with achievement. In the air which shares us,
who is telling who?
'I flew, Papa, I flew!'
'I know, child, I know.'

The bright side of the coin is wonder, the way children have of disappearing entirely into a game, a garden, mud, whatever the moment is made up of. Their curiosity propels them forward. Their wonder at the variety of the world keeps leading them deeper into it, to the point where they find themselves suddenly lost and, just as suddenly, afraid. As we comfort their fears, they reward us with delight. In exchange for the promise of a future, they give us an awareness of the present.

Obviously, children have not been long enough in the world to have a past; and, just as obviously, the future, however they think of it, is something still so remote and inexplicable as to remain for them only wishful. There is no alternative for them but to *be*, to be in whatever circumstances the day offers. The idea of making plans never occurs to them, for they are obliged to accept, like it or not, the plans made for them by others larger and more authoritative than they. Thus, unencumbered, they are able to give their full attention to the present, the day they find themselves alive in, the place they happen to wake in. It is all they have.

To us, wonder is more elusive, since we have entered into responsibility, either as parents or simply as self-sustaining human beings, to the extent that wonder, or wondering, seems an indulgence, if we ever evade the press of time. It may be that we avoid wonder. It is not exactly comforting to feel our selves, our identities, our whole existence, called into question. But, this fear aside, we are still caught at odd moments by the astonishment of a painting, a reflection, weather, the taste of food, any vivid displacement. In such moments we see how habit and familiarity have clogged our direct awareness, and muffled our spontaneity. It is as if we cannot afford the luxury of getting lost; and yet, getting lost in moments of wonder is, perversely, what we most value.

Wonder evades a definition, precisely because it is the high point of awareness *beyond* language. We must return from the intensity of it and attempt to express it in verbal analogies, poems and the like which will make it *happen* rather than try to describe it. Wonder begins when we disappear *into* awareness, when the seer and the seen become one, when we *realize* rather than recognize. Later come the categories and the language. Children are prone to wonder because they are in fact seeing many things for the first time; and they do not yet have in their heads the conceptual mechanism for explaining them away. They wonder because they do not yet understand. We are luckier in that we can go back from a conceptual understanding to recover our wonder—if we have not forgotten or are not reminded, what it is.

What is interesting is our own preoccupation with anything that can induce in us the sense, which, we are aware, has been diminished by habit, of an endless present—Zen Buddhism, hallucinogenic drugs, dabblings with the occult. These pre-occupations are only a sign that we are cruelly aware of a kind of slavery to time, and are ready to grab at anything which might free us.

Waking up, we wake, at least momentarily, into the same unknown that children inhabit, until we put on responsibility as we dress. There is no point in our trying to tell children how lucky they are, for they would have no idea what we were talking about. Enough to take wonder when it occurs to us, catching, when we can, the strange wave-length of children.

Language. Faced with terrifying natural happenings like thunder or lightning, primitive peoples allayed their fear of them by finding a name for them, so gaining power over them. At the same time, the mystery of the happening passed into the name, and made it magical. Much the same thing happens with children, as they learn to name things and, so, cease to fear them, mesmerized at the same time by the magic inherent in words. To get hold of a word like 'balloon' or 'bumblebee', to say it over and over, becomes a hypnotic delight, a pure joy. In the village in which I grew up, there was a butcher with the name of Coid. I used to repeat that name to a point of ecstasy, and it still delights me, even although I have forgotten the butcher and everything about him. For children, words are both a game in themselves, and a way of playing with reality, of manipulating it, of juggling with it. Quite apart from saying anything at all, sheer saying is a pleasure in itself.

Children learning to read. To break through this enormous sound barrier is for them consistently magical. Painfully, they spell out, piece together, and ultimately pronounce a word which they suddenly realize they already know, and which refers to an object which is already part of the furniture of their world. We, on the other hand, have been using language so long and so indiscriminately, that the magic has long gone. That is why, in teaching children anything at all, we generally learn more than they do. For us it is rediscovery, which is doubly affecting.

Once I had learned to read, I began to take all kinds of journeys, through books which I did not begin to understand, but which, because they were made of words, were quite enough for me. I read, with equanimity, things that should have terrified me. I devoured a pictorial history of the First World War with zeal. But once in a while, a phrase, a sentence, a line from a poem, would leap out, would hover in my mind, and would haunt me beyond any explanation, beyond sound, beyond sense, in the way that some poems still do. I read children's books, to be sure, but only because they kept being provided. I never thought of them as any different from other books, except that they were rich in pictures. Although I have written a handful of books for children, it would not surprise me to find that children had no interest in them. We choose books for children which we think they should read; but, as with most of our attempts to recover our childhood, we under-estimate the appetite children have for language and pictures far beyond their understanding, but well within their wonder.

Magic. I had a remote uncle whom we visited once a year, at Christmas, and who was renowned among us children for one incredible facility he had—that of blowing pennies from where we sat to any part of his vast house we chose (or imagined we chose), under the grandfather clock, in a book in the library, on the stairway leading to the attic. The penny was always there, just where we, or he, had said. Each time we were weak with wonder, and pestered him for penny after penny, and eventually, for the secret. He was wise enough not to tell us (and indeed, to this day, I am not *quite* sure how he did it). But as we grew older, we were only interested in *how* it was done, and, denied any explanation, we wandered away. When we were younger, however, that he could do it at all was awesome, and magic was a perfectly satisfying explanation.

The power of pretending. Without thinking, children change their surroundings at will, into whatever shape or substance they would like. At any moment, unaware that they are doing it, they are able to make a garden into an entire universe, to become pirates, animals, giants or even plants without any difficulty. We may envy this, for *we* have discovered the world to be more intractable.

For children, to lie is not always an attempt to deceive, to conceal, or to save their skins. Very often, a child lies because it *wants* its own fiction to come to pass, and feels that there is a faint, magical chance that it might. It is not easy to decipher a lie, since it might in certain cases be better classified as a work of the imagination.

> *Mother, I went to China this morning.*
> *The trees were pagodas, the puddles were seas.*
> *Dragons were hiding behind the begonias.*
> *I was a mandarin.*
> *Willows were bowing.*
> *Lies, lies, said she.*
> *And I hid from her frightening eyes.*
> Who can say, who can say?
>
> *Children, the gardens belong now to goblins.*
> *The willows spread legends, the waterfall plays.*
> *Fairytales wind like a web round the window.*
> *Goodnight to all birds now.*
> *The night's wings are folding.*
> *Lies, lies, said I.*
> *But I hid from her wonderful eyes.*
> Who can say, who can say?

I suppose that it is easier for adults to speak to children than for children to speak to adults. Adults, they like to think, can adapt themselves to the tiny wave-lengths of children, to make themselves understood by a kind of transference that is quite often more wishful than real. Children, on the other hand, are limited to their own stunted vocabulary, and are overcome by the agony of making themselves understood. The truest communication between adult and child takes place outside language, when they are united suddenly in laughter, or in wonder.

Eavesdropping. Listening to children talking to themselves is far more revealing than listening to their direct conversation. Talking to themselves, they give free rein to both their fear and their wonder. The conversations they invent with their own ghosts are far less inhibited than those they hold with us. The ghosts, the imaginary playmates, as they know better than anyone, cannot answer back. There is nothing to fear.

I am not sure at what precise age children acquire a sense of time. I only know that it is somehow the beginning of disaster, or at least the beginning of growing up. For children, to-morrow is just as remote, just as inconceivable, as next year. Wondering about something which has not happened yet has nothing to do with wondering over the amazement of something in the moment. And yet, as we grow, the landmarks in our lives begin to move, faster and faster, until they are whizzing past us like telephone poles. The reason children have such difficulty in learning to tell time is, quite simply, that time is of no interest to them.

Jean Piaget, in all his articulate researches into the awareness of children, keeps pointing up the fundamental conflict— between the egocentricity of children, and the enormity of the world around them, both human and physical, which is persistently claiming their attention. The needs of a child are imperative. The requirements of the outside world are equally imperative. The whole complexity of growing up is one of finding a tolerable balance between these two imperatives. Children, in their egocentricity, insist on being satisfied. The world, outside of them, does not insist, but is irremovably there. Hence, growing up is a matter of walking a tight-rope and occasional casualties are not surprising.

What we suffer from is an infinity of possibilities, all of which we can imagine happening to us, between which we are constantly forced to choose, and because of which we become anxious and afraid. Possibilities scarcely preoccupy children, except as a game; for them, actuality is all.

A child is caught in a perpetual struggle between its isolation and its connection with people, things and language. On both sides, fear lurks—on the one side, the fear of loneliness, of being lost, on the other side, the fear of a welter of unknowns. What we call experience is a process of becoming familiar with enough of human life to be relieved of our fear of it, to be able to cope with it. Familiarity, if it does not breed contempt, certainly breeds dullness. The conflict which the child has between its isolation and its connections never entirely disappears. Considerably later in life, isolation dawns on us all over again. Since, by that time, our capacity for wonder has subsided, our real fear, the fear of death, is not easily consoled. Except possibly by the presence of children. When, in those rare moments of sudden unspoken astonishment which we share with a child over something seen, felt, heard and realized, all at once, there is no such thing as age, no such thing as time, no fear, no isolation—only the awe, fearful and wonderful at once, in the here and nowhere of the moment, at being alive at all.

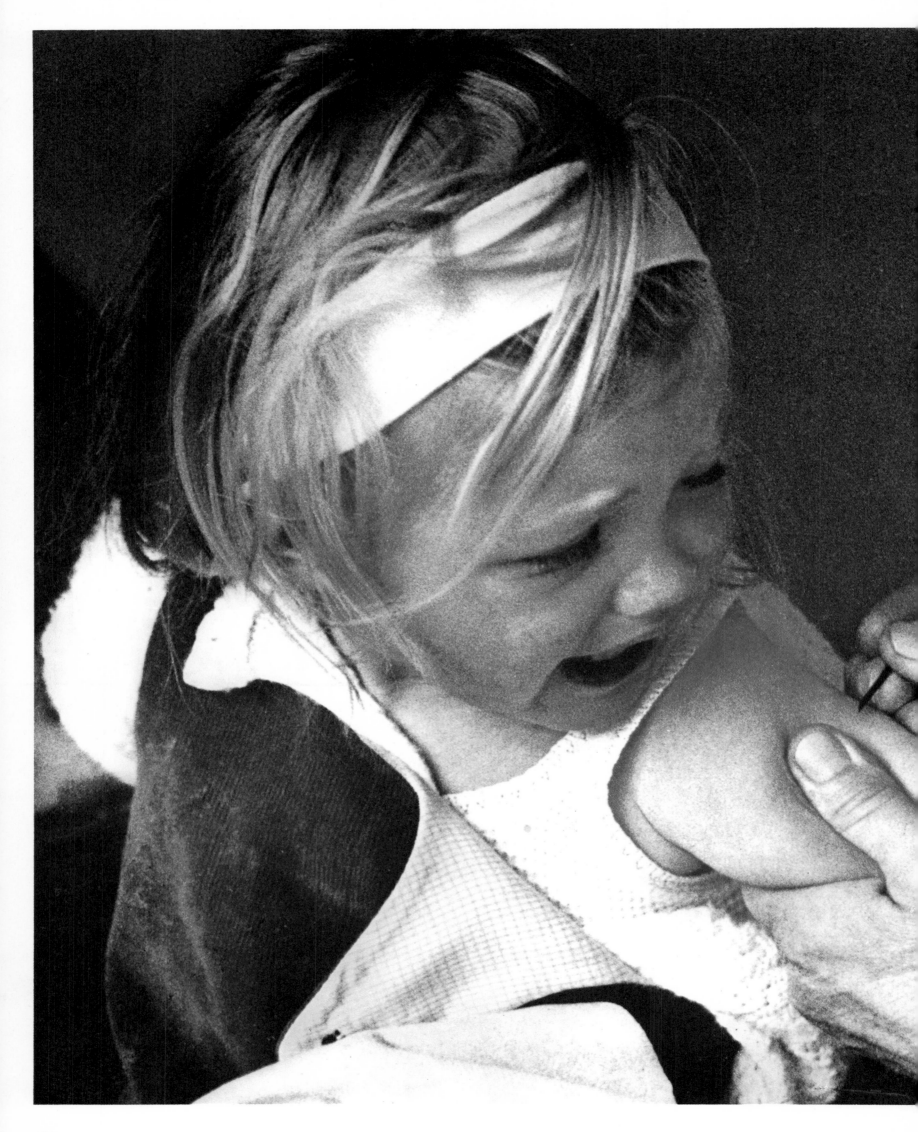

Will it hurt?

The world is full of terrifying things. Steamy hot water suddenly bites the hand put under a kindergarten tap, a strange man wants to poke a hole in your arm, a street dog rumbles menacingly.

179

A universal remedy

If the sea sounds too big and feels too wet, if a hammer has treacherously smashed your thumb, if a bully has grabbed your ball. There is only one cure—to reach out for, and find waiting, a grown-up hand.

Little girls lost

Tears and dismay when lost in England (left) . . .

. . . a clutch to keep from being left behind in Trinidad (right).

Friend or foe?

In a Vietnamese village children show both fear and wonder as soldiers suddenly stride into town after a Vietcong attack. Will these huge creatures bring good things to the village, or bad?

The two faces of the law

The Johannesburg policeman (below) instinctively reaches for his notebook when he sees two villagers coming into town on market day. All Africans entering town are required by law to carry passports, and the police have a reputation for being most unpleasant when this law is not obeyed. So the African boy and his mother have reason enough to be afraid.

186

To the girl on Brighton Beach in England, this officer of the law is a most helpful fellow. He is taking her to the Lost Children's Bureau. But wherever they are, most children very sensibly fear policemen, because they are powerful and mysterious.

What is it?
Does it move?
Is it real?
Can I touch it?
Will it bite me?
Can I take it home?

188

ANACONDA.
EUNECTES murinus.
South America.
Purchased.

Outsiders and insiders

A display behind plate glass provides
South African street boys with a
tantalizing look at unobtainable toys.

A bedroom window in Paris is a show case in which this two-year-old French girl must be content to view the forbidden outdoor delights of a rainy day.

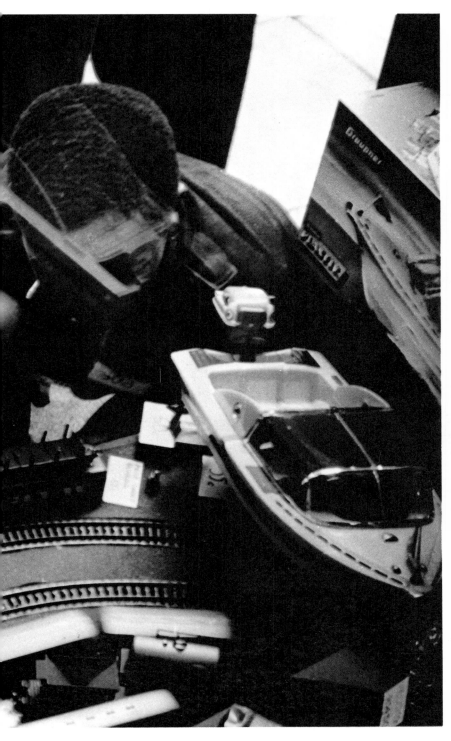

Ballooning fancies

. . . The Tuileries, Paris.

. . . Luxembourg gardens, Paris.

. . . Macy's Thanksgiving Day
Parade, New York.

. . . New York World's Fair, 1964.

193

Playing with fire

In reflective silence children at a London party consider the magical flash and hiss of newly lighted sparklers.

Stretching out her hands, a Bavarian girl reaches for the fiery confetti of a New Year's sparkler.

Clenching her teeth for courage, a New Zealand tomboy carves a blazing pattern in honour of Guy Fawkes.

'Christmas comes but once a year'

At Christmas time children are confronted with a world for once almost equal to their capacity for wonder. For them, toys in big department stores are not so much future possessions as the rich accoutrements of an imaginary world whose infinite possibilities cannot be limited by troublesome parent or frightful price tag. The only frightening figure in the Christmas drama is the department store Santa, who laughs a little too loudly, sweats more than he should and keeps adjusting his false beard. It is only good sense, therefore, to approach him, like the little English girl opposite, with a proper mixture of hopeful awe and protective hauteur.

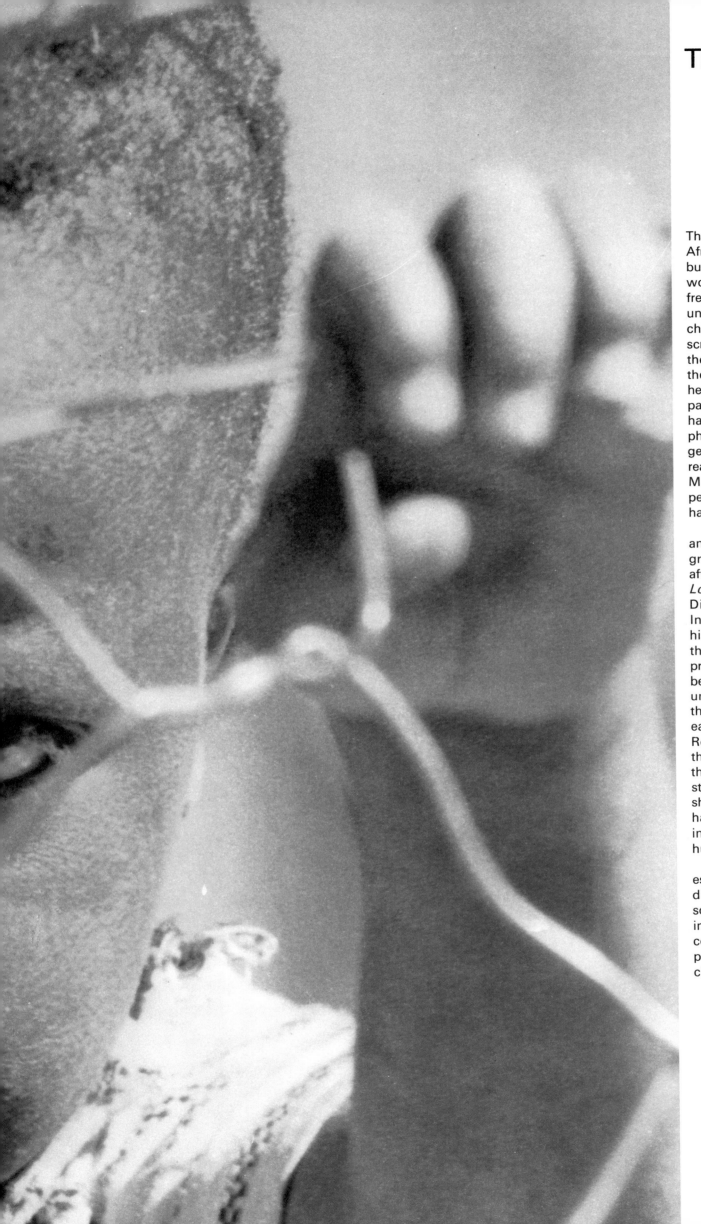

The Hostile World

This sad-faced boy lives in an African township near Johannesburg. He looks out towards a world where there is greater freedom than his own. It is not uncommon to see pictures of children who live a life circumscribed by wire. But nowadays there is greater concern than there once was. Whether we can help them or not, for the most part we care about what's happening to them. And when a photograph like this evokes genuine concern it is surprising to realize that, not very long ago, as Marghanita Laski shows, most people would have taken the hardships of a child for granted.

Miss Laski, novelist, journalist and critic, and the mother of two grown-up children, was described after her famous novel *Little Boy Lost* as a writer 'akin to the Dickens who wrote of children'. In this chapter she traces the history of the harsh usage given the young, whether by way of profit, pleasure or politics, from before the time of the Spartans until the present. She reminds us that even today, long after the early days of the Industrial Revolution, or, for that matter, the final days of Hitler's Germany, the young still suffer cruelty in a startling number of ways. And she shows how their treatment has been reflected, historically, in changing attitudes towards human life, the law and religion.

The accompanying picture essay records some of the disturbing instances where, in a society that we assume is increasingly civilized and compassionate, the world still presses heavily on the lives of children.

199

'Cruelty has a human heart . . .'

Marghanita Laski

'Do you hear the children weeping?' asked Elizabeth Barrett Browning, and by 1843, when her poem 'The Cry of the Children' appeared in *Blackwood's Magazine*, no civilized person of sensibility would have denied that he heard. But it had been for only a comparatively short time, for something like a hundred years, that children had been accepted as proper objects for special pity, and we must start by asking whether we can fairly speak of a world hostile to children during centuries when it occurred to hardly anyone that children, as children, should arouse compassion. We must trace the growth of pity before we can speak of hostility.

Some people—not all people—have always loved their own children, as the Old Testament amply shows. Yet we shall find small concern there for children as such: 'Happy shall he be, that taketh and dasheth thy little ones against the stones,' sang the Psalmist of the Babylonian enemies. Nor shall we find much compassion for children in that ancient Hellenic world which we often assume to have been the cradle of our virtues. Someone might write a touching epitaph for his own child or a child he knew, but the pity is for the survivors:

Philip's Nîcotelês, a twelve-year lad,
Lies buried here : the hope his father had.

There is deeper compassion in an epitaph for a dog:

We called him Bull : he went into the dark.
Along those roads we cannot hear him bark.

There are no dirges for the new-born babies whom the Spartans exposed for hardihood's sake and the Athenians, when besieged, against starvation. It was long before the days of that Hellenism which Matthew Arnold saw as the source of sweetness and light when Homer spoke for the fatherless child in tones that seem to reflect some of our own sensibilities:

The day that robs a child of his parents severs him from his own kind; his head is bowed, his cheeks are wet with tears, and he will go about destitute among the friends of his father, plucking one by the coat and another by the shirt. Some one or other of these may so far pity him as to hold the cup for a moment towards him and let him moisten his lips, but he must not drink enough to wet the roof of his mouth; then one whose parents are alive will drive him from the table with blows and angry words. 'Out with you,' he will say, 'you have no father here,' and the child will go crying back to his widowed mother.

But the voice of Homer found no echo for many centuries; and nor did the next noble voice which spoke for the children, the voice of Jesus, yet it was his vision of the child in a hostile world which, some seventeen hundred years later, became our own.

Let us recall what he said, for it is of great significance, and appears in more or less similar form in three of the Gospels. In the Matthew version (chapter xviii), we read how the disciples came to Jesus asking, 'Who is the greatest in the kingdom of heaven?'

And Jesus called a little child unto him, and set him in the midst of them, And said, 'Verily I say unto you, Except ye be converted, and become as little children, ye shall not enter into the kingdom of heaven. Whosoever therefore shall humble himself as this little child, the same is greatest in the kingdom of heaven. And whoso shall receive one such little child in my name receiveth me. But whoso shall offend one of these little ones which believe in me, it were better for him that a millstone were hanged about his neck, and that he were drowned in the depth of the sea. . . . Take heed that ye despise not one of these little ones . . . it is not the will of your Father which is in heaven, that one of these little ones should perish.

But not even the disciples, in those days, accepted this part of their master's message. It is in the next chapter that we hear of little children being brought to Jesus that he might lay his hands on them and pray, and of the disciples rebuking the children; and it was then that Jesus spoke the words on which today people of goodwill, of all religions and none, try to act:

Suffer little children, and forbid them not, to come unto me : for of such is the kingdom of heaven.

We in our own century cannot but amazedly ask how it was, with their master's words unequivocally before them, that Christians did not, through the centuries, hear the cry of the children. The answer is that doctrine forbade it.

It is only for a very short time that Christians have ceased to insist, not on the innocence, but on the natural depravity of the child. For the child is conceived in sin. He is born unregenerate, redeemed only by the grace of Holy Baptism, likely always to lapse and fall. 'What wast thou, being an infant, but a brute having the shape of a man? Wast not thy body conceived in the heat of lust, the secret of shame, and stain of original sin?', and, again, 'Iniquity is connatural to infants, and they are more prone to Evil than to Good, we must not therefore indulge them too much.' Thus Lewis Bayley and John Pechey, writing the one at the beginning, the other at the end of the seventeenth century in England, and they express the common attitude to Christian children throughout the first seventeen centuries of the Christian era.

Inevitably this world was harsh and hostile to children, but hardly anyone felt it to be, and when Pope Gregory, seeing the English slave children for sale in the Forum at Rome, commented compassionately that they looked like angels, not Angles, his unusual response became part of recorded history. In telling the story today we lay more stress on the Pope's pity than on its objects, little commodities of that ever-flourishing trade, slavery, and perhaps it is salutary for us in England to recall that English children were not slaves only because harsh conquerors forced them to be. William of Malmesbury, the twelfth century historian, tells us of the pre-Conquest English:

There was one custom, repugnant to nature, which they adopted : namely, to sell their female servants, when pregnant by them and after they had satisfied their lust, either to public prostitution, or to foreign slavery.

In 1005 a law was passed by the Council of Evesham, forbidding the selling of Christians 'beyond the bounds of this land, or at least not unto heathen folk'. The law left loopholes enough. Slavery, either under its proper name or such others as serfdom or villeinage, was long common throughout

Europe, dying in England only in the fifteenth century, in France in 1789, and in many other countries later still. Throughout our era many more children must have been born, grown and died bond than free.

It is rather people than specifically children whom we must pity during those many hundred years, for life was equally horrible for all of them. If the little children froze in the fields in winter picking up stones, burned in the summer scaring birds from the crops, this was only the earliest stage of lives literally nasty, brutish and short. Where parents lived horribly, children lived horribly, as they almost always must. Where children could be usefully employed, with profit to someone, there existed no known reasons why they should not be so used. Even very young children could tend poultry, dip rushes in tallow for lights, comb wool. They could be trained for entertainment by the jongleurs and jugglers who thronged the roads, as later by theatres and circuses. They were among the rogues and vagabonds who lived by fleecing the public, for a small child has always many special uses in crime; we recall little Oliver Twist pushed through the scullery window so that he could admit Bill Sikes by the street door. And in the early days of industrialization children had many uses. Thomas Deloney, the Elizabethan novelist and ballad-writer, breaks into doggerel to describe a weaving manufactory in Newbury:

Within one roome being large and long,
There stood two hundred Loomes full strong . . .
By every one a pretty boy,
Sate making quills with mickle joy . . .
Then to another roome came they,
Where children were in poore aray :
And every one sate picking wool . . .
The number was seven score and ten,
The children of poore silly men :
And these their labours to requite,
Had every one a penny at night,
Beside their meat and drinke all day,
Which was to them a wondrous stay.

Jack of Newbury was a good employer who cared for all his hands. Deloney, his chronicler, obviously saw these one hundred and fifty working children as fortunate, and so, for the times, they were. He would have agreed with Thomas Fuller who wrote in his *Worthies*, some sixty years later, of the lace-making children of Honiton: 'Hereby many children, who otherwise would be burthensome to the parish, prove beneficial to their parents.'

To us, the absence of a special compassion for children in these decent, generally kindly men may seem extraordinary. But pity was not withheld from the children of only the poor. For the children of the rich, too, the world was usually hostile and loving-kindness rare. We must recall the child marriages of royalty and nobility which often entailed a child of very tender years being sent away among strangers. The English upper classes have long been held to care little for their children, sending them away from home at early ages, whether once to other noble houses to be trained in upper-class expertise, or, later, to boarding-schools for the same

purpose. Schools were stern, discipline strict, yet often no stricter than at home. Let poor little Lady Jane Grey speak for the children whose parents were unkind. She was telling Roger Ascham in 1550 of the years before she was sent away from home when barely nine. Only four years after this conversation took place, when sixteen, she was beheaded:

When I am in presence either of father or mother, whether I speak, keep Silence, sit, stand, or go, eat, drink, be merry, or sad, be sewing, playing, dancing, or doing anything else, I must do it, as it were, in such Weight, Measure, and Number, even so perfectly as God made the World ; or else I am so sharply taunted, so cruelly threatened, yea, presently sometimes with Pinches, Nips, and Bobs, and other ways (which I will not name for the Honour I bear them), so without measure misordered, that I think myself in Hell.

Before the enlightenment, many a child must have thought himself in hell. But only a very few people—and Roger Ascham, who recorded Lady Jane's words, was among them—thought it wrong to treat children harshly, or envisaged a world in which it could be otherwise.

Why did so great a change in human sensibility take place, a change as revolutionary as the invention of romantic love at the end of the eleventh century, about which C. S. Lewis has written, 'Real changes in human sentiment are very rare— there are perhaps three or four on record—but I believe that they occur, and that this is one of them.' I myself believe that another of these real changes in sentiment is the change in the attitude to the child that came about in the eighteenth century in western Europe, and that it is only after pity was established as morally desirable, that we can fairly speak of hostility.

I have posed the question, Why did it occur? only to have to admit that I cannot answer it. More usefully, I must explain what it consisted of and how it came about.

What happened is that the child, from having been (as we have seen) naturally evil, an imp of Satan, conceived and born in sin, became, as Jesus had seen him, the type of those most fit to enter the kingdom of heaven, naturally innocent, pure and good. As Adam and Eve before the Fall, so the child became a symbol of innocence, goodness and purity in a naughty world.

In England we find the first significant stirring of this attitude with the coming of the eighteenth century. Undoubtedly John Locke's treatise *On Education*, published in 1693, focused a new popular interest on the child (as witness the second volume of Richardson's *Pamela*, of 1741), but probably the most significant beginning was a satirical one, Jonathan Swift's *Modest Proposal for preventing the Children of Poor People from being a Burthen to their Parents or the Country*. As is well known, Swift's Proposal was that instead of leaving children to starve they should be fattened and eaten (George Bernard Shaw made a similar proposal, much later, when he suggested we should preserve children as we do pheasants and shoot them in season, thus leaving many more alive and nourished). But few people respond to savage satire, and more widely significant was Thomas Coram's founding of the Foundling Hospital in London in 1739. Before that, children had been among the inmates of the various hospitals, leprosies, charitable schools, founded by the Church and later by laymen. Here, for the first time in England, came a charitable institution specifically for destitute children.

Satirists, practical philanthropists—and then, most influential of all, those unacknowledged legislators, the poets. First, William Blake, with his *Songs of Innocence* published in 1789, the year when across the English Channel, substantially influenced by Jean Jacques Rousseau, another believer in the child's holy simplicity, the French Revolution flooded the world with concepts of freedom and compassion. Pity the child who sweeps chimneys, cried Blake, pity the lost child, the charity child, the corrupted child, the drunken child, the infant slave.

> *Is this a holy thing to see*
> *In a rich and fruitful land,*
> *Babes reduced to misery,*
> *Fed with cold and usurous hand?*

The place of the children, pleads Blake, is not the chartered streets, the satanic mills, but the Echoing Green where the birds sing and the children can play in carefree, cherished happiness. But there is no Echoing Green, and the children suffer. 'Are such things done on Albion's shore?'

Such things were indeed done, and it is horrible that in this period, when the flood of compassion for suffering children moved a few people to a new agony of pity, the children of England suffered probably more cruelly than ever before.

Wordsworth's Immortality Ode gives us the child of the idealists, the pure unsullied infant trailing clouds of glory, growing ever further from heaven as the wicked world corrupted and imprisoned him, and Wordsworth's attitude is probably still that of most feeling people today. But when he wrote, the new upsurge of feeling affected comparatively few. The Industrial Revolution was far more potent.

It was the Industrial Revolution in England that immeasurably worsened the lot of the children. The little chimney sweeps, the little drunkards, the deserted children were terrible enough, even if it was only now that some people began to realize how terrible they were. But work in the new factories and in the mines was far more horrible than in the old manufactories or the fields, life in the new octopus-sprawling slum towns more hopeless than in even the decaying rookeries of the old country-encircled cities; and the new chimneys were narrower than the old ones. Both work and life were now more horrible for everyone, child and adult, but our concern is with the children.

> *The increased employment of children was largely due to the fact that mechanical inventions had opened out new means of utilizing child labour. Employers soon found that children could do much of the factory work; and children were plentiful at a penny a day. They were often swept into factories when they could hardly walk. The Poor Law authorities of London began carting off waggon loads of pauper children to Lancashire.... Children of eight, seven, or even six were frequently employed in factories. It needed more than average enlightenment and self-sacrifice to keep them at home or at school till they were nine; and the poor little mites often had to work twelve or thirteen hours a day. The condition of many of the factories was disgusting. The atmosphere was often abominable; the moral atmosphere sometimes worse. Children of both sexes were growing up in a sort of slavery, broken in health and brutalized in mind.*

This general picture is from the late-Victorian historian H. D. Traill. One can multiply detail indefinitely. The 1841 Select Committee found that in the lace-making industry the children often did not go home for twenty-four hours at a stretch. The Mines Commission of 1843 reported that children of three were being employed, and that children and women worked 'chained, belted, harnessed like dogs in a go-cart, black, saturated with wet, and more than half naked, crawling upon their hands and feet, and dragging their heavy loads behind them—they present an appearance incredibly disgusting and unnatural'. The evidence given before the commissions makes reading nearly as ghastly as reports of the atrocities of our own times. Here is some of the evidence given to the Sadler Committee on conditions in textile mills in 1832 by a woollen worker whose own children worked in the mills:

Q. Do you not think that those children were generally treated more cruelly at the termination of the day, when they have over-laboured themselves, and are actually fatigued?
A. Yes.

Q. Is it not found by universal experience that the most cruel punishments take place when undue hours of labour are imposed upon the children, and when, therefore, they are no longer able to perform the work?
A. That I have been a witness to. I have seen some slubbers [textile workers] encouraging them to sing hymns in order to keep awake; others would be beating them about, and throwing things at them to keep them awake.

Q. When a child gets three shillings a week, does that go much towards its subsistence?
A. No, it will not keep it as it should.

Q. Do you receive any parish assistance?
A. No.

Q. Why do you allow your children to go to those places where they are overworked?
A. Necessity compels a man that has children to let them work.

Reform, despite compassion, was slow. The novelists added their voices to the poets', Mrs Gaskell for the north-country factory folk, Charles Kingsley for the chimney-sweeps and the industrial workers, Dickens for most of the social tragedies of the age. But profits were for a long time more powerful than pity. The first attempt at a factory act in England was in 1802, the Health and Morals of Apprentices Act, which was to limit the child labour of parish apprentices—but not of children sent to work by their parents—to twelve hours and in the day-

A scene in modern Britain—filthy children caged in a dirty crib. For the law it is often difficult to judge when parental care has lapsed to a point that justifies official action. Among various agencies that become involved is the independent National Society for the Prevention of Cruelty to Children which aims at improving conditions of children in the home to at least a tolerable level. The Society's latest records show that in one year 325 inspectors and home visitors saw 114,641 children. In an astonishing 39,223 cases, parents later had to appear in court.

time; the Act was totally ineffective since it included no provisions for inspection or penalties for evasion. By 1842, after ceaseless campaigning, notably by Lord Shaftesbury, children under ten were excluded from the mines, but only slowly, and not until the third quarter of the century could it be truly said that the worst evils of child labour had in some fields been abolished. We may however care to remember that the last of the English boy chimney-sweeps died, an old man, in 1949.

When the worst cruelties of the English Industrial Revolution had been overcome, children were far worse off than they had been before it, for they had been brutalized and corrupted, in body and in mind. Many, like Dickens's Jo in *Bleak House*, had never known family life. Some lived in gangs (like the Russian children after the Revolution, and the European children after the last war), sleeping where they could, dressed—if one can call it dressed—in rags, stealing to keep alive. If they were caught, they could not expect mercy. In 1833 a child of nine was condemned to hanging for stealing five halfpence worth of paint.

Throughout the nineteenth century and almost up to our own times, one could not look at the children of the poor without horror and shame ('Are such things done on Albion's shore?'), and this despite the great Christian revivals of the first half of the last century. Child labour continued, breaking through loopholes in the law. In the poorer districts as well as the rich, domestic servants were employed right up to the First World War, and in the poorer districts these servants were often children, the so-called 'half-timers' or 'partial exemption scholars', who were allowed, after attending school for half the day, to work not more than twenty-seven and a half hours a week for not less than three shillings a week, and only if over twelve years. But in outraged Fabian pamphlets we hear of much younger children working longer for less, of a girl of six, for instance, who worked for twenty-nine hours a week for twopence a week and her food; and this was after the turn of the century.

The blunt facts were, as they nearly always have been, that where children were profitable, they were used; where they were not, they were neglected, apart from the efforts of the small but evergrowing body of reformers. Three fields in which profits have long been made out of children were education, prostitution and drink.

Dickens's picture of Dotheboys Hall in *Nicholas Nickleby* can stand as exemplar of the so-called Yorkshire schools, where for low fees children received starvation diet, harsh treatment and no education worthy of the name. To these were sent the children that parents wanted to get rid of; and to some, the children whose parents believed that boarding-schools conferred social superiority. There are still 'Yorkshire schools' in many parts of England today, and in other countries too.

The prostitution of children of both sexes has long been common in many parts of the world, and notably in the East. Among English Victorian vices was the debauching of very young girls. The novelist Michael Sadleir, whose books were always adequately documented, has given us a description of such a child in *Fanny by Gaslight*:

It was a shrimp of a child, with staring eyes set in a face which showed the dead pallor of fright even under smears of rouge and kohl. On the forehead was an angry bruise. Instead of being dressed in a child's frock or (as would have seemed more likely still) in rags and tatters, the little creature wore a grotesque parody of a grown-up evening dress. Made of a white taffeta striped with pink, sleeveless and with a deep décolletage, the garment hung by two straps on the meagre shoulders and fell forward over the child's flat chest, exposing it to the navel.

The satisfaction of this vice, which included the sale of children overseas, especially to Belgium, was not checked until 1886 when the age of consent was raised to sixteen, after the notorious case in which the journalist, W. T. Stead, was imprisoned for buying a child without its father's consent. This he had done, with the co-operation of Bramwell Booth of the Salvation Army and Mrs Josephine Butler, to show how easily it could be done. In previous attempts to protect young girls by less melodramatic legislative means, gentlemen concerned to protect their peculiar pleasures provided some of the nastiest examples of hypocritical selfishness in all the sordid history of trying to save children from greed and cruelty and exploitation.

But the story of children and drink provides some nice examples too. Obviously, the more people who drink, the more profitable to the brewers. It is true that in early days children drank beer and that it was probably safer for them than the contemporary water; but the beer was mostly home

Hitler killed two million Jewish children in Europe. These two small boys were among his victims. With thousands of other Jews they once lived within the square mile called the Warsaw Ghetto. They were surrounded by a wall ten feet high, crowned with barbed wire and broken glass. Their daily rations sank to a tenth of what was needed for normal nourishment. In 1943, arms were smuggled in by the Polish underground. In April fierce fighting began. A month later the Germans had burned the ghetto to the ground and taken 56,065 captives, not counting the four thousand who died in the flames.

brewed, and there was small profit to be made from it. It was a different story when it came to the monstrous gin debauches of the seventeenth and eighteenth centuries, and many a child was, with its elders, drunk for a penny and dead drunk for twopence. But after sensibility to children's suffering arose, there was constant concern to save children from the ravages of drink, throughout the nineteenth century and well into our own.

In 1833 a committee was set up in England to investigate the workings of the Beer Act of 1830 which had given the right to sell beer to anyone who paid an excise fee of two guineas; nearly all of these sold spirits as well. Here is an extract from the evidence:

Q. You have mentioned that a great number of children as well as others entered the shops on certain days; what is the average age of those children?
A. I should say, from six to sixteen years of age.

Q. Can you state whether the children went in to drink spirits or to fetch spirits for their parents?
A. According to my observations, I think about half went in without bottles and the other half with bottles.

Q. Can you state the smallest quantity sold to children?
A. They have penny glasses.

Mr E. S. Turner, in *Roads to Ruin*, writes that 'A considerable revolution in thought had to be effected before the sight of a tipsy child, seeking to slap its prostrate parent back into consciousness, could be regarded as a subject for pity rather than for fun.' What the brewers could do to retard this revolution they did, and some often surprising members of the public stood behind them, like the Bishop of Peterborough who stated, in 1871, 'It would be better that England should be free than that England should be sober.' But despite his and similar protests, it was, in that year, made illegal for children under sixteen to be served with spirits, though they could still drink beer in public-houses. The next move was an attempt to prevent any child under thirteen from buying any kind of intoxicating liquor; if this were passed, said opponents desperately, it would mean that parents would have to go to pubs themselves to fetch their own beer. But the reformers had some telling evidence to bring, of infants suckled on gin and rum, of a two-year-old alcoholic in hospital sobbing for porter, an eight-year-old boy with delirium tremens. Such stories did not prevent the Liverpool brewers from sending a deputation to the magistrates, asking that the age at which children could be served with spirits be lowered from thirteen to ten, or publicans in Birmingham, Manchester and elsewhere from enticing children into pubs with sweets. But gradually the children were protected—in 1901 by the weak act known as the 'Anti-Sipping Act' which insisted that bottles sold off-licence should be (albeit ineffectively) sealed, by the so-called 'Children's Charter' of 1908 which made it illegal for a child under fourteen to enter a bar or for a child under five to be given liquor without medical authority, this last because many infants had been doped or made drunk to stop them crying. Finally came 'Lady Astor's Act' of 1923, which governs the position in England today.

But if, here and there, the unceasing efforts of reformers eased the position of the children, the ravages of the Industrial Revolution were not easily cured in a period when profits were still more important than pity. The price England paid in the destruction of English children became clearly visible with evacuation for war in 1939, and the facts were set out in print in a shamefully neglected book, *Our Towns*, published in 1945 by the Women's Group on Public Welfare. Here it is reported that in the London County Council School Medical Officer's Report for 1937, only twenty per cent of the infants could be considered as having good homes; that a substantial number of children billeted not far from home were never visited by their parents, and some deserted for good and all; many had been used to going to bed at late, irregular hours, and some had never slept in a bed; swearing was common, even in very young children, so was lack of respect for people as for property; many children lacked nightwear or even a change of underclothes; many had lice, nits, such 'dirty' skin diseases as scabies, impetigo, ringworm; there were bed-wetters and soilers, some who deliberately soiled curtains and furniture, others who soiled beds and clothing through never using toilet paper. Bodily dirt was common, so were dietary habits and deficiencies likely to cause poor health. Indeed, in 1938, a study of nutrition among schoolchildren in Birmingham classified only two and a half per cent as excellently nourished. The Industrial Revolution, whose ravages were worse in England than in any other country, had set up a vicious spiral of squalid family life which had hardly been effectively broken by 1939—we do not know how far it has been broken today—and ignorance, poverty, slum living, had taken almost as drastic a toll of the children of one of the most civilized countries in the world as it still does among those who have not known civilization's benefits.

Against this tragedy of rot and decay, it would seem unfitting to say much about the harshness endured by children economically and socially more fortunate. Many, we know, were still brought up with cruel repressiveness; the new attitudes are still far from universal. Many were unloved; some children always are unloved, among rich as among poor. But generally speaking, by the early 1900s (a period in which, among the poor, malnutrition was, as J. C. Drummond wrote, 'more rife than it had been since the great dearths of medieval and Tudor times'), the children of at least the well-educated middle classes in England were probably as fortunate as any in the history of childhood, the most cherished creature in the home, the heir of the ages, whether cosseted as a plaything for its supposed innocence, or laden, as in many high-minded and progressive families, with the duty of helping to create a new clear-eyed uncorrupted world that should be an Echoing Green for all of us.

So far our tale, if melancholy in substance, is nevertheless a cheering one. Where life is hostile to all, children will seldom be specially protected—and life still is hostile to all in most of the world. But we have seen that the civilized world, if usually harsh to most of its citizens, shows promise of improvement at least to its children and, in some areas, performance as well as promise. Where opportunity offers, there will always be some who will exploit children, as they will exploit adults, for profit. There will always be parents who do not love their children, or do not love them enough to sacrifice their own immediate pleasure or benefit. There will always be those brutes, usually parents, who treat children with sickening cruelty, and the poor, as we were reminded a long time ago, we have always with us. But if some cannot respond to the change of feeling which sets up the child as our chosen symbol of innocence, more and more are able to do so and will respond to cries for help, not only from our own children at home but from strange children far away.

It is, then, the more terrible that near to the close of our story of the hostile world we must recall a tale of cruelty worse than the world had ever known before, the cruelty inflicted on children by the Germans from 1933 until 1945, and whose ravages long endured.

Why was this the very worst? Children had been massacred before, even, quite recently, in Britain, in Glencoe in 1692. Children were wantonly slaughtered in the Allied saturation bombing of Dresden, and at Hiroshima and Nagasaki in 1945—and perhaps this was nearly as evil as anything the Germans did. Children in England and in America are frequently despised, if they are not white Anglo-Saxon Protestant males, for belonging to another than the Master Race. Children are lost, orphaned, wounded, freezing, starving, killed in many parts of the world today.

I think that the German destruction of children (and of adults too) can fairly be considered the worst because it was the act of a people who previously had known and accepted standards of civilized behaviour. Odd as it may sound to say so, the cruel treatment of children in England during the Industrial Revolution, till then the worst, was incidental, not deliberate. It was simply more profitable that way. What happened in Germany was intended.

Perhaps the first child victims of Hitler could be considered the Nazi youth, the generation of boys whom he trained to callous obedience, the girls brought up for breeding. But this iniquity pales beside the treatment of children not German. There were the sixty-one children of Lidice in

These two pictures, as vivid as film stills, seem strangely theatrical now. A quarter of a century ago, when they were taken, they were intensely real, part of an organized hostility that threatened children all over the world. The strutting Nazi boy, giving his Heil Hitler salute, was one of the children who were brutalized unknowingly by the cruel society they belonged to . . .

Czechoslovakia of whom only fifteen were ever found, the children of Oradour in France burnt alive with their mothers. Two million Jewish children died. Of the 4,363 Jewish children deported from Belgium only thirty-nine returned.

The children died in various ways. Some were used as labourers until worn out. Some were frozen to death in the deportation trucks. The inmates of several children's homes simply disappeared. Some children were used for medical experiments, some were shot, some infants were swung against walls. Some were killed, in mercy, by their mothers. Some died in the gas chambers.

But some children survived. Of these, there were girls of ten with venereal disease. There were children who did not know their family names, and there were blond children adopted into German families, appalled to learn that they were Jewish. All over Europe children had learned to lie and steal and pander as the price of survival—a Dutch psychiatrist said, 'It was dreadful to watch how quickly and how completely the children became depraved.' Almost all the surviving children were in poor health, some irretrievably

crippled in body or mind. Almost all had lost irreplaceable years of education. These children, this sick, corrupted, ill-educated, demoralized generation, accustomed to the foullest cruelties the mind can devise, are today's younger Europeans.

A hostile world indeed, a hostile self-destructive world, laying up for itself in each generation legacies of hatred and incapacity. What can we hope from adults who have never lived, as children, in the loving, secure homes which, we now know, are the only backgrounds that can produce the secure, well-adjusted adult?

If only we could feel that this orgy, this holocaust of cruelty had caused such a revulsion of feeling that wanton cruelty to children by whole nations could never occur again! But we cannot. If, among individuals, compassion is slowly, steadily growing—and individual support, and notably that of children themselves for such organizations as UNICEF, is impressively moving—nations in pursuit of their own ends seem as thoughtlessly brutal as ever. Children are being bombed (incidentally and accidentally of course) in Vietnam. Coloured children are being denied full education in Rhodesia

... this terrified boy is one of the millions whom the Nazi child was conditioned to hate—a Jewish boy being rounded up for slaughter in the Warsaw Ghetto in 1943.

and South Africa. In almost every civilized country of the western world children are living below the poverty line.

Nor can we all be confidently sure that the new would-be sciences believed to benefit children have in fact brought kindness rather than cruelty. With astounding readiness (it may seem to history with insane readiness) western intellectuals have proved ready to accept the notions of theoretical psychology, to regard the newborn infant as arriving not in clouds of glory but burdened with birth trauma, obsessed with dank dark memories of the womb. The 'six years' darling of a pigmy size' no longer lives, as Wordsworth saw him, among 'new-born blisses' but is agonized with the effort of repressing incestuous desires for his mother, murderous impulses against his father, hatred for his siblings and the sombre stirrings of lust. We may perhaps hope for some redress from the newer findings of experimental psychology, from Dr John Bowlby's discovery through the research he did for the World Health Organization that the infant's major need is for love from his mother, and from recent suggestions that a loving father plays an indispensable part in later years.

But the earlier myths seem to be dying hard, and they carry many incidental cruelties with them, such as the over-anxious semi-informed parents' perpetual search for symptoms of psychological irregularities in their offspring, and the often intolerable freedoms forced for self-expression's sake on children who long to be safely bound by rules. Too much love was never so burdensome as too much dubious understanding and too much unwanted, terrifying freedom.

And always, there are the incidental accidental cruelties, forever finding new forms. Perhaps life in the cramped urban apartment block high above the ground with no play-space, no meeting-ground close at hand, is the most characteristic of our age.

To have learned—for only some of us to have learned—to pity children was a great step forward. To continue to confine our pity to children would be mawkish if not perverse. The change in sentiment that took place in the eighteenth century when we began to hear the cry of the children must be no more than the first step towards a world in which nearly all of us are able to feel compassion for nearly all human beings.

Taking no chances on the unknown

A shepherd boy in Ethiopia, two small girls fishing in north-east Thailand—and in both cases the questioning stillness invoked by a stranger. Where they live any stranger is a threat until proved otherwise. The reaction is natural enough in vast stretches of Africa and Asia where superstition is widespread and life is so often shaped by flood, famine, sickness and the other inexplicable hostilities of nature.

Almost anywhere on the African continent a boy like this one can be found. He has been put out with some sheep or a few goats. The sun burns down on him and he may rest fitfully under it for hours in the same few square yards, his toes flexing in the accustomed dust. His ragged dress is a usual sight. So is his amulet—the beads put round his neck to ward off evil. And so are the festering sores on his raised arm. They are a sign of yaws, a widespread sickness that children, if they stay strong enough, usually outgrow.

The Thai girls live in a village in Korat province. The long, dry season, which follows the heavy rains, has begun and they are fishing for food in large pools left behind by the flood.

209

Beg, borrow and what tomorrow brings

Two Vietnamese orphans at the Saigon racetrack. They are aged four and six and are already professional touts. Shuffling familiarly through discarded betting tickets near the betting booths, they try to sell the lottery tickets they have brought with them. In their short lives Vietnam has been steadily at war. An openly hostile world, which has left them superficially unmarked, may have marked them totally. Meanwhile they are simply trying to get enough money to buy rice.

Saigon has many such children, partially cared for, existing in chaos. Sometimes they have parents to instruct them in their begging. Sometimes, parentless, they are directed by older children. There are no official orphanages. A few homes, run by American women, can attack the problem only at its fringe.

Urchins have learned that the racetrack, where the public has money in its pockets, is the best spot to cajole, plead and pester their way past the indifference that most adults develop in a city full of beggar-children.

Tiny, shoeless, not yet three, this Negro boy in Johannesburg is too young to say very much. But he already knows all the words for the trade his family has put him to. He, probably like them, is a beggar, part of the South African scene, where many thousands plead in the streets or go from door to door asking for bread or work.

As in any country with a vast number of poor, this boy will be clothed and fed only if he, or his family, succeed at the one job they have found to do. From grown-ups, as he grows up, he learns to expect the rejection that shows on this white man's face. If he is not too weak or sick, it may toughen him and arm him better for his trade.

Is home where you happen to be?

Salford is a dank industrial town in the north of England. This girl, who lives there, is not hungry. If you are hungry and there is no sun, you do not lean on cold, iron lamp-posts in Salford. She holds a meat bone because she likes the company of dogs. The dogs have finally left her because she has teased them with the bone and decided not to give it to them. She lives in a grimy, unpleasant result of the industrial revolution. The cotton mills of Salford, like others similar to them, once exploited children hideously.

For a girl like this, though the town may be oppressive, it is exciting. It has given her a tough-girl look and a tough-girl attitude. She has a house and a family to go to. In some undoubting way, she belongs to the town and feels at home there.

The boy has been waiting in a long line and now stretches his hands up to the bars of an office window—to get something to eat. He is a refugee, a Palestinian Arab in Jordan. His home is a camp where every day he waits hungrily like this for a meal-ticket from the United Nations Refugee Welfare Association. The ticket will get him his daily three pennies' worth of food.

Jordan's refugee camps hold 137,000 people; many more have been assimilated into new homes in the country. Though he doesn't yet understand his predicament, this boy, like all refugees who stay alive, has grasped what he must know and do to go on existing. But however well he learns the routine of the camp, whatever techniques he acquires for survival, he will never be at home there, will never, unlike the girl in Salford, feel on home ground.

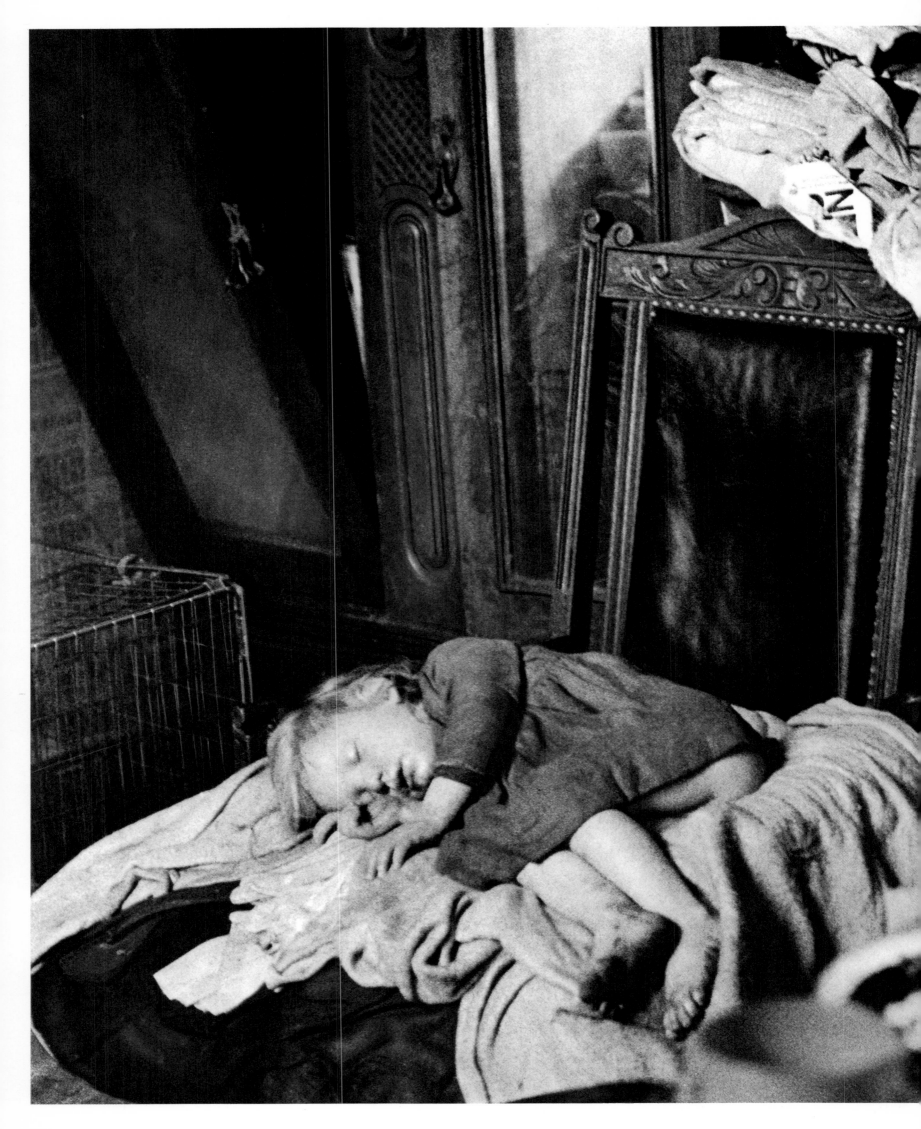

No place like home

You can dream of princes and toys in a room like this, or of anything else, probably. This child undoubtedly knows the taste of welfare-state orange juice, just as she knows that milk comes from a bottle stuck amid clothes and papers on the sideboard. She is given cooked food. There is virtually no chance that she will physically starve.

What will happen to her mentally is less predictable. She will be educated by the state to at least an elementary level. But how will she learn to cope with the effects of living in a kind of theatrical chaos?

Childish reflection of a grown-up conflict

This is a stoning. The stones will sting and maybe cut, but there have been worse stonings. There is not much anger here, and the black children are almost jocular as they throw. The scene is a dirt road by a placid reservoir in the Northern Transvaal. No one is going to be killed here—not now anyway.

Michael Joseph, the photographer who took this picture, watched the whole fight. He saw the white boy start it, behaving with the South African white's sense of supremacy. What there was of underlying malice was kept largely in check, for all these children have already learned, apparently, that uncontrolled temper,

in South Africa, is like a stone in a pool. One angry incident can spread into a riot.

Perhaps what these boys are engaged in is some sort of rehearsal for the future. Behaving as boys have always at times behaved, they are mirroring the attitudes of a more intense conflict which they will inherit.

216

The beginning of adversity: active and passive

This is an English home and no face is smiling in it. It has neither the room, nor the vitality to support the sort of rough and tumble that is occupying a gang of American boys in Philadelphia. In Britain, half a million people live in overcrowded houses—two people to a room and often more. Clutter and passivity grow together. The walls press in and a sort of homogenized squalor grows until the people who live in the midst of it no longer know how to deal with it. Outside, the world is more ordered and going out can become an ordeal. To wait inside is easier and gives the illusion of security.

In the open air, on a vacant lot in Philadelphia, a sudden hostility boils into a fight. Baseball is forgotten for a while as two boys roll in the dust while their seven supporters shout, smile, identify with one fighter or the other. The chances are it won't last long. Then they'll all play ball again. Just the same a fight is frightening— and it isn't a form of play.

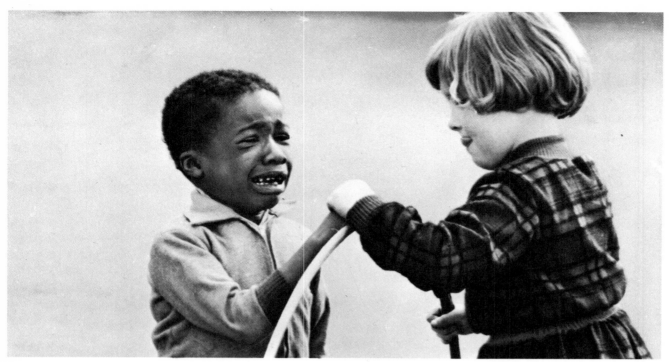

Growing pains

Confrontations come in all sizes, starting pretty early in life. A child can talk back, fight back, run away or stand. Or, perhaps, just begin to cry. He may grow up to be a coward, a bully, a hero, a pacifist, a diplomat. But whatever he is, it is likely that memories of how he behaved in some childhood squabble will often please him, haunt him, even shape him.

The boy at left in the playground at Leicester in England is clinging to a school hoop which he was handed out to play with during lunchtime. His adversary is a girl whose job it is to collect all the hoops for the teachers. The boy's tears and struggles do no good. He is learning the pangs of being up against official rules—and an opponent who out-weighs him heavily.

The boy in the wintry street in New York's Harlem doesn't much want to fight. He doesn't want to run either. His fists are up but they are slack, less than half-clenched. But most of the story is in his eyes. He is afraid to hurt or be hurt. In any case by having to fight he is learning two things—an enemy and his own doubts.

The enduring legacies of hunger

This little boy in India is sitting contentedly in the sun savouring a biscuit given him as a handout by the Indian government. Through earlier malnutrition his shoulders have become pitifully small for his head and it is already too late for the care that has produced the biscuits to help him very much. He needed care from the cradle, but is one of the six in every ten Indians who do not get enough proper food. And he is one of the 25 per cent who are just not getting enough food of any sort.

Another victim of malnutrition, a boy who was born mentally deficient because his mother was so short of food, crouches in a yard in an asylum in Quito, Equador. He is one of 850 defectives confined in a 200-year-old building that has never been improved. The Sisters of Charity who run it tend the inmates with kindness but little equipment or medicine. In a poor country the patients are given mercy but no real hope of a cure.

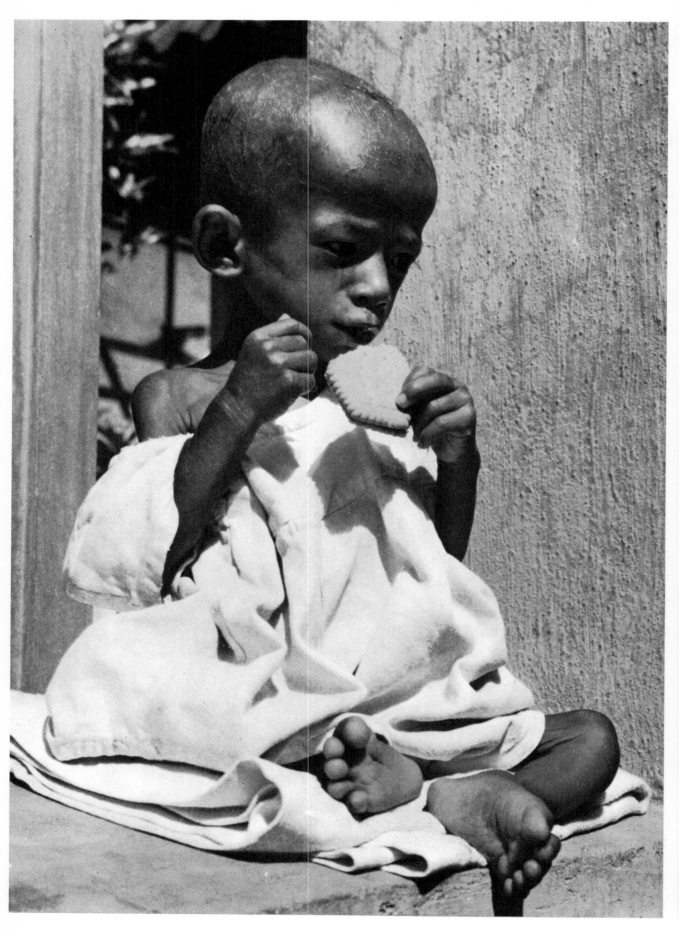

The loneliness of the mad and the fearful

Isolated in fear and ignorance, a Maku Indian woman in Brazil bathes her sick child after treating him with lighted nettles. The boy has been stung by a scorpion and will surely die unless this magic can prevail. His sister watches, and learns, the ritual. The mother will draw the nettles four times across the child's body, bathing it with water in between. Then they will wait by the fire, for as long as it takes.

Alone in his madness, a boy sits like a lump before a cathedral in the island of Majorca, ignoring the jeers of three boys who cling to railings. They have just rattled the metal to try to stir him up, but have now lost interest. He is an imbecile, well enough clothed, physically cared for, but left like a vegetable in the sun before the cathedral, just to pass the time. Spain has been improving its facilities for treatment of mentally handicapped children lately, though the handicapped are still worse off there than in much of the rest of Europe. But the incidence of mental handicap is no higher in Spain than elsewhere. In most of the world's countries, about one family in five has a member suffering from mental sickness and about one person in 400 is mentally handicapped.

The Shaping Spirit

'If God made everything, who made God? What is at the edge of space? When is "now"?'

These are the questions of a child trying to make sense of the world. Traditionally children's existential why's have been answered by formal religion. But are these really answers? Are there ever any answers to the riddles of existence? Dan Jacobson, author of the following essay, called *Riddles of Existence*, has listened closely to the questions children ask and has found them to be the same 'embarrassingly childish questions' that men of genius continue to ask throughout their lives. He is not surprised that parents find these questions difficult to answer, and he asks a question of his own: Is it true that children *need* to believe in a god?

It seems likely that formal religion of some sort will always provide necessary and consoling answers for most people. The pictures accompanying the text of this chapter, which show children taking part in religious life all over the world, are a reflection of the regard for religion as life's shaping spirit.

But the original phrase 'the shaping spirit' is Coleridge's: 'What nature gave me at my birth. My shaping spirit of Imagination.' For Coleridge this vital, growing poetic imagination was a mighty creative force, mirroring within man the creative power of God. For children, imagination is the key to a secret world of their own. The pictures which complete the essay portray various aspects of that world. What magic is practised there and what wisdom is learned no one knows. Everyone who tries to describe it runs an acute risk of becoming a sentimental bore. Still, everyone is tormented by a suspicion amounting almost to a faith, that inhabiting and creating this world, children are somehow closer to the mystery of existence than anyone else.

Riddles of existence

Dan Jacobson

'ALL SUFFERING MUST CEASE.'

This plea or command, written in carefully inked block capitals on a piece of drawing paper, was pinned up on the wardrobe of a girl of about eleven years old, the daughter of some friends I was visiting. She was a pretty, reserved, watchful child with bright eyes and a fringe of black hair across her forehead, and was lying on her bed and reading when I blundered by mistake into her bedroom. She was acutely embarrassed when she saw that my eye had fallen on the notice; I was sufficiently embarrassed by it not to remark on it, either to her or to her parents. But it was not a notice that one could easily forget.

'If God made everything, then who made God?'

I was asked that question by a five-year-old boy. It sprang out of nothing that had been said by anyone in the preceding conversation; his mouth was full of food at the time, and one would have thought the problem of cosmogony (as I think it's called) to be the last thing his mind was preoccupied with at this moment.

When I was about fourteen years of age . . . a necessity I could not understand swept over me: I had to try again and again to imagine the edge of space, or its edgelessness, time with a beginning and an end or a time without beginning and end, and both seemed equally impossible, equally hopeless—yet there seemed to be only the choice between the one or the other absurdity. Under an irresistible compulsion I reeled from one to the other, at times so closely threatened with the danger of madness that I seriously thought of avoiding it by suicide.

That is a quotation from Martin Buber's *What is Man?* There is no need for us to doubt the truth of the experience as he narrates it, or to imagine that only a child who was to become an eminent philosopher would undergo a torment of that kind. (Though it is pretty certain only a future metaphysician would have found an answer to his problem as the young Buber did: he was much reassured, he tells us, by a reading of Kant's *Prolegomena to all Future Metaphysics*, which he 'dared' to go through in spite of the fact that 'its first sentence told me it was not intended for the use of pupils, but for the use of teachers.')

The four-year-old son of a couple of thoroughgoing rationalists once told me, with a troubled, rambling, repetitive earnestness, the story of the Fall of Man, in terms which he seemed to have invented almost entirely by himself. A long, long time ago there had been a good place, which he called simply 'The Green', where almost everybody had lived; outside it there were a few bad people ('Robbers'), who were always trying to get into The Green. Finally, one of them managed to slip into it, and he drove out the good people. Ever since then the good people have been looking for it, but the Robbers get in the way and make sure they'll never find it.

From my own childhood I can remember at the age of about nine a preoccupation with time, which, though I can hardly call it obsessional, for it was almost pleasant or entertaining in its teasing quality, nevertheless kept me awake night after night. The preoccupation took two forms. The one was simply to ask myself: When is 'now'? Now? But by the time I had said it the moment of saying it was already past; when I was thinking of doing it the moment was still in the future. Could I never arrive at 'now-ness', and what would it be like if I did? The other, related form the preoccupation took was a wonder at the fact that our actions were, strictly speaking, unrepeatable; we could never do the same thing twice in exactly the same way.

I would, for example, press my thumb against my forefinger, then open my fingers, and then press them together again. The two actions appeared to be exactly the same, but how could I be sure that they were—that the degree of pressure I had exercised the second time was exactly the same as the first; that exactly the same areas of skin had met each time; that the rest of my body had not altered its position between the two actions? In any case, even if, *per impossible*, my actions were identical in every respect, so that not even the finest instruments could have measured any difference between them, the fact remained that my actions had taken place at different times, no matter how closely they had followed upon one another, and the total contexts of each thus differed immeasurably. The world had turned a certain distance, I was so much older than I had been, people who had been doing one thing were now doing another . . . and so I would be led back either to the riddle of what we meant when we said 'now', or to a general, vague speculation about the outward largeness of the world, its inward complexity, and the utter incomprehensibility of either of these two directions opening before the imagination. Fortunately, both directions led in the end to sleep—another incomprehensibility, doubtless, but one by its nature more soothing than the others.

Some years later I found myself burdened with a preoccupation or worry that had nothing pleasant about it at all: at the age of thirteen I confronted with much surprise and even more resentment the idea that death was absolutely unavoidable for everyone in the world. I had not suffered a bereavement of any kind, so the astonishment I felt was not directly personal; it did not—at least, so far as I remember it—even spring from a fear or horror of death itself. No, what seemed to me absolutely insupportable was simply that there was no getting around it. You could live to be a hundred and twenty. Doctors could invent all kinds of medicines and serums. You could be the King of England or the President of the United States. Still, in the end, you would die. Everyone now alive would die. I felt it to be intolerable that we should be so completely overruled, that it should be made so brutally plain to us that our wishes, our will, our achievements and our individuality counted for nothing.

Finally, as a way out of this humiliating condition of impotence, I adopted a programme of what I felt to be inner, unassailable defiance—though I took care to see that it never became more than an attitude, a last resort hidden safely and silently inside my own head. We were *not* slaves to death, I said to myself, like some stumbling, backveld, adolescent imitation of a character out of Albert Camus, as long as we had the freedom to die by our own hands. This reflection made me feel much more cheerful; indeed, by that time I had

meaning of evil, the nature of evolution and the nature of death. Buber's torment was paraphrased for me in the simplest terms by my eight-year-old son: 'How can space just go on and on?' he asked—and then: 'But how can it stop? What's on the other side if it stops?' What indeed? 'Where was I before I was born?' 'If you went on counting where would you get to?' 'I don't like thinking about space—it makes me feel funny inside.' 'Is there a God for the people on Mars?' 'What *happens* to all the dead people?' 'God *must* be true because . . .' 'God *can't* be true because . . .' 'Sometimes I believe in God and sometimes I don't.' 'How do I know what's really real and what isn't?' We have all probably made such remarks and asked such questions; or have had them made to us and asked of us. And later, in adolescence, we have decided that life is meaningless because 'it's all just molecules in combination', or is not worth living because 'more people are unhappy than are happy'; or we have been challenged by adolescents to rebut such statements, if we can.

But one of the great differences between children and adults in this regard is that children live in the hope that if they really work at such problems, if they really concentrate all their strength on them, they will be able to resolve them, they will come upon final answers. Even the gloomiest of adolescents arriving at the conclusion that there is nothing more to the world than molecules in combination is convinced that the truth he has come upon is permanent and unalterable, that it will always be with him; this is precisely what makes him so gloomy. Considering how overwhelming to a child is the impact of the sheer physicality of the world around him— how fresh and extraordinary all its sights, sounds, textures and smells can be—it may seem remarkable that there should be so much interest in and responsiveness to such abstract wonders as those I have mentioned above. But, as many people will be able to bear out, the child does not feel such wonders as abstractions at all. It is not merely that they arise from the attempt to make some kind of order out of the physical world so pressingly around him, but that they themselves take the form of sensations and emotions as much as of thoughts. Dizziness, claustrophobia, a godlike feeling of expansion and command, breathlessness, luminosity and darkness, fear, awe and fatigue—all these can be the rewards and penalties of trafficking with the most remote of intangibles.

By the time the children have grown up, on the other hand, they have become so pessimistic about their own capacities, and so daunted by the nature of the problems they were once impelled to tackle, that for the most part they simply choose to think about them as seldom as they possibly can. (Which is one of the reasons why, when one reads the work of men of genius as dissimilar, say, as Pascal and Tolstoy, one of the words which come inevitably to one's mind in describing them both is 'childlike'. Neither of them was prepared to stop asking himself the most embarrassingly childish questions. 'Why am I here,' Pascal asks, 'and not there? Why now and not at another time?' In one of the greatest moments of one of his stories Tolstoy puts this indignant reflection into the mind of his leading character: 'Caius was certainly mortal, and it is right for him to die; but for me, little Vanya, Ivan

argued myself into a position where my decision to go on living did not appear to me an act of prudence. Having made, as I thought, a conscious choice in the matter, I felt it to be positively heroic.

Any reader will, I am sure, be able easily to add from his own experience to the few examples I have given above of the 'metaphysical' or 'philosophical' speculations of children. Some readers, too, will confirm that such speculations took up more time in their childhood, and were pondered over with a deeper, more wholehearted intensity than they have ever been granted subsequently. Children, in fact, seem to me to be natural metaphysicians, preoccupied more frequently than most of us care to recall with the ends and essences of the most mind-wrenching abstractions—God, space, time, life, eternity, infinity, numerical recurrence, the

Ilyitch, with my thoughts and emotions—it's a different matter altogether. It cannot be that I ought to die. That would be too terrible.') Furthermore, apart from the fact that they have to earn their livings, provide for their inquiring children, keep up with their friends, and follow the news and a multitude of other diversions, grown-ups today are confirmed in their distaste for metaphysical speculation by what they hear, from a distance, about the main tendency of modern philosophy. That philosophy, everyone is pleased to gather, has dismissed all inquiries about the 'ultimate' nature or purpose of any abstractions as strictly meaningless (at least until language can be rendered precise enough to deal with this problem). Pascal, Tolstoy and all the children have been wasting their time.

Each generation sees little but its own obsessions in the minds of its children. So a sceptical, positivistic, smutty age chooses to forget what it was like, when one was five or ten or fifteen years old, to make the effort to find final answers to the greatest of all intellectual and moral problems, or at least to be absorbed into the wonder of them. Instead, it gratefully sets about the task of finding evidence for the genesis of its own constant sexual busyness in what the children do and say.

Thus—to use two of the examples I have already given—the little boy's story about the Fall of Man is clearly his version of the birth trauma; or it is (with an equally self-evident clarity) his expression of his jealousy of his father's sexual opportunities and activities, his father being the Robber who gets between himself and his mother's much-desired Green. And that is that. Again, the girl who wished for all suffering to cease is almost certainly disturbed by the first dangerous pre-pubescent stirrings of a more alert sexuality than she has ever known before: those are the sufferings that she really wishes to see coming to an end. Such interpretations come far more naturally and happily to us than an admission of the possibility that, in the first case, the child is trying to make sense of a world which simultaneously offers him so much pleasure and so much to fear; or, in the second, that a girl of eleven could perfectly justly find unendurable her vivid imagining of all the evil and pain which exists everywhere in the world.

But surely, I can hear the protesting voices go up (my own among them, I confess) I am not going to suggest that children are without sexual interests and passions; I'm not going to fly in the face of sixty years of psychoanalysis. No, I am not. Far be it for me to touch a single grey hair on the head of that infant prodigy among the sciences. What I am going to suggest, however, is that the sexual curiosity of children is in itself linked more closely than we are often prepared to admit to curiosities of quite another kind—to their curiosity about the genesis of the world and of all living things; their curiosity about the nature of life and its place in the cosmos. They want to know more than we can ever tell them when they ask, 'How was I made? Where do babies come from?'

But before continuing with this point, it is, I think, only fair both to psychoanalysis and the children to say that anyone who has ever observed children, or can remember much

A Bar Mitzvah ceremony, in which a Jewish boy, at the age of thirteen, formally acquires religious responsibility and knowledge of the Law. Guided by the rabbi, the boy reads from the Torah, while his father (left) and grandfathers (right) look on.

A young Buddhist monk contemplates the universe from a field near Khon Kaen, Thailand.

of his own childhood, must find it difficult to believe that there ever was a time when it was imagined that children before the age of puberty were bland, innocent, sexless, neutral creatures. Was there really ever such a time? The books seem to tell us that there was; but the evidence of our own eyes goes right against it. We are forced to believe either that children have changed their nature, or that parents were once singularly unobservant, or that the books were just not telling the truth. Of the three possibilities I would unhesitatingly settle upon the last.

We can, it is true, argue whether or not it is right to call children's interest in their own bodies and that of everyone else 'sexual'. We can deny that their fascination in the process of excretion be given that name. We can insist that a delight in being cuddled, kissed and fondled is 'innocent'. But after all our arguments, denials and insistences, we are still left with the difficulty of finding any other word to describe so many of the activities, the demands, the games, the word-play, the questions, the unconscious, rhythmic movements of children practically from birth until they arrive at the age of puberty. From then on they may know more directly and certainly than ever before what it is about their bodies that has made them so restless (and the effect of this conscious knowledge, of course, is often to make them shyer, more estranged from themselves than before). But it seems to me undeniable that puberty is not the emergence of a totally new force within them, as it used to be spoken of, but the sudden, startling development of one they have always had.

However, let us go back a few years—back to the relatively unselfconscious child asking his parents where he came from. Let us say that his parents are of a conscientiously modern and enlightened kind, and in reply they give him, as rationally as they can, a brief account of 'the facts of life'. (The phrase is in itself one that could do with a closer scrutiny than it usually receives.) Such accounts, I know both as a child who once received them and as a parent who has given them, are never really satisfactory. The first, most obvious difficulty with the facts of life is that they are so implausible. It is a far cry indeed from what the Freudians call a child's polymorphous sexuality to his being able to find it credible that the sexual act ('the making of a baby') can be anything other than a gratuitous, utterly irrational absurdity, a self-evidently foolish thing to do. By the time he reaches puberty he will, inevitably, have been instructed by his peers and by every shrieking cinema poster that there is nothing else in the world that can begin to compare with it in magnificence and importance; his (or her) own body will do the rest for him, eventually. But in the meantime the abyss of puzzlement and incredulity remains and is made to seem all the wider by the restrictions and shames which, from the time of earliest toilet-training onwards, are always associated with the organs of reproduction.

But it is not only their inherent unlikelihood which makes the facts of life, as we pass them on, so puzzling to most children. It is also their incompleteness. They ask us 'How?' but they also want to know 'Why? To what end?' Now I have no doubt at all that it is far, far better for parents who have no answers to such questions to make it plain that they have no answers, rather than to trump up explanations in which they do not really believe. If words like 'life' or 'instinct' or whatever limp alternatives to them we are able to offer, are vague and difficult for children to understand, they do not seem to me much more so than 'the will of God'. At the same time we should, as parents, and as ex-children, have the grace to be modest about our own ignorance, rather than scornful of the children's demands and anticipations. We should remember that the child's pressure towards the ultimate explanations we cannot give him and he can never attain is itself the growth and working-out of a human instinct as imperious as any other.

But what about God? Is it true, as people often say, that all children need to believe in a god of some kind, and that hence the simplest, most reassuring thing any parent can do is to refer their children's inquiries direct to God? (This was a point of view repeatedly and emphatically put forward by George Bernard Shaw, I remember, in all his writing about the upbringing of children.) My answer to the last part of that question would be that only parents who are in fact believers are entitled to make such a reference—the others, as I indicated above, must struggle on as best they can. Children are not easily fooled, and unbelieving parents who adopt insincere postures for the sake of their children will be seen through very quickly. So the ultimate effect they achieve would be the reverse of reassuring.

As for the 'need' of children to believe in God, or a god, the truth seems to me that one finds among them the widest variations of scepticism and belief about the strangest collection of deities. These variations are not only to be found between one child and the next but within the same child at different times. There are children who devoutly believe in God at the age of five and not at all by the time they are ten. There are probably more children still, at almost any age, who are sceptics by daylight and believers after nightfall, when sinister shadows gather in corners of rooms and at the ends of passages. Quite apart from the more or less orthodox instruction they may receive from parents, ministers and schoolteachers, and which they then re-interpret for themselves as vividly as their vocabularies and imaginations permit, they are capable of making gods—sources of infinite power, knowledge and danger—out of electricity meters, cans of food with particularly numinous patterns or designs on them, pieces of furniture, pictures, trees and a host of other objects. It is a fine point whether supernatural presences of this kind should be called gods or demons; everyone who has spoken to me of having had some such object of worship in his childhood has never remembered it as a benign or altogether trustworthy force. Or rather, even those who did have wholly 'good' gods to serve never were without 'bad' ones as well, which could emerge out of the cracks in a ceiling, the sound of the wind in a gutter, or a collection of rubbish in a darkened corner of a garage. As in some Nordic myth, these gods were always at war with one another, and the outcome of the battle depended greatly on whether or not the unfortunate child caught in the middle carried out the duties imposed on him by his worship. One of the most stringent of

these duties almost always appears to have been the observing of a strict silence about the whole dangerous affair.

All this I am reporting from what has been told to me by others. My own religious experiences as a child were of so limited a kind that, hearing of the terrors and raptures experienced in the childhood of people more prone to worship than myself, I feel rather like a tone-deaf man being told about the rewards of listening to music. I had a perfectly vivid picture of God in my mind, formed in the most commonplace way by Scripture lessons and Bible stories, as well as by visits to our local synagogue: God was a rather benevolent-looking old man, with a pointed white beard and some sort of black, sacerdotal headgear on his head. Around him, in circles, were stars, angels, blue spaces, mountains. He held in His hand the tablets of the Law, as they had been given to Moses. This picture, as I say, was vivid and constant, it altered very little over several years. The trouble with it, however, was that I just did not believe in it; it was never for me a representation of what really existed, either physically or spiritually. I was never tempted to pray to it, or to imagine that such a figure could help me through my fears and puzzlements. Nor did it have anything to do with my ideas of good and evil, or right and wrong—I think the notion that these had to have supernatural sanctions in order to be really effective would have bewildered me greatly. The commandments of morality were quite strong enough as it was, without any extra reinforcement from above. The penalties for disobeying them were not merely the certainty of angering parents or other grown-ups, but also the pangs of an ever-present and ever-active guilt.

In this respect I do not believe my feelings were at all out of the ordinary: my impression is that childhood, so far from being a blithe, innocent, amoral or pre-moral time of life, is in fact the time when the burden of morality weighs most heavily and unambiguously on the consciousness. One can almost say that it is just for this reason that morality is not a 'problem' to most children in the way that God or death or sex are problems. It is only as they grow older that they come to realize that there are conflicting moralities in the world, among which they have to choose, that adults who are always ready to issue moral precepts frequently fail to live up to them, and that the existence of the moral sense they have previously taken for granted is yet another mystery to be confronted or avoided. For children the problem of morality is whether or not to obey a moral code of whose existence they have no doubt; which is quite another state of mind and feeling from that in which most adolescents and adults find themselves, especially in a time like our own age.

With the single exception of the problem of morality, I would say that the questions touched upon here are those which change least in their form and substance throughout the span of one's life. What does change is our individual attitudes towards them, and also the attitudes which society in general encourages us to adopt. We have no alternative but to pass these on to our children, as we pass on all our other skills and ignorances. But our children are there to remind us of what we sometimes prefer to forget: that our attitudes are not, and never can be, answers.

Their secret world

'Then stirs the feeling infinite, so felt
In solitude, where we are *least* alone'
—Lord Byron

Artistic impulses, felt in solitude. Poster paints mixed in mother's patty tins. Brushes washed in the baby's potty—all in a Johannesburg garden.

Recollections in tranquillity—poetry begins on the improvised hammock of a plank stretched between two oil drums.

The magic circle

Her secret world can be the cot which has encompassed all her earthly possessions for as long as she can remember, or a hula hoop on the kitchen floor, inside which she drags all her favourite toys. These are the physical limitations of this first precious society-of-one. A circle, as the ancients knew, is magic because it has no beginning and no end and is complete in itself.

'Read, mark, learn and inwardly digest'
—The Book of Common Prayer

Left: Owlishly devouring the 'British Trades Alphabet 1964' a student takes time off from studying Greek at an Oxford prep school.

Right: Perched in the crook of a cherry tree, a South African reader tries to make sense of the strange lines and squiggles.

Two's company: a world to share

Two small boys put their heads
together, the better to peer down a
grill in the Dublin pavement.

In the centre of a Lagos market, but
oblivious to its noise and bustle,
two African boys enjoy the intimacy
of a rubbish dump.

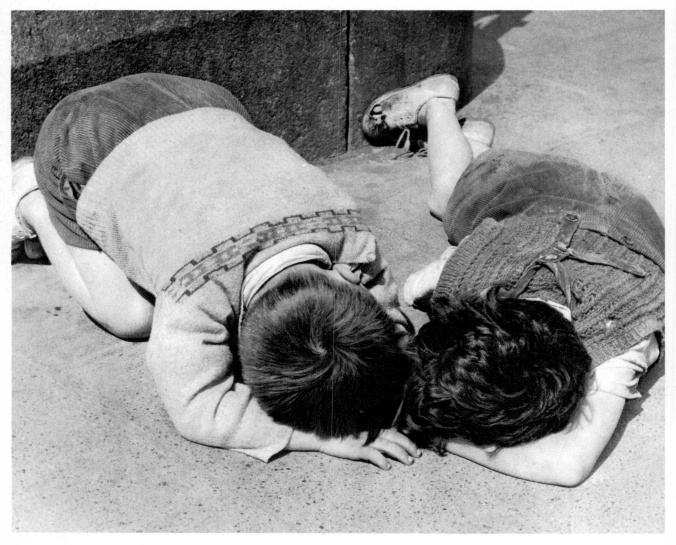

'Know you what it is
to be a child? . . .
It is to believe in love,
to believe in loveliness,
to believe in belief . . .
it is to turn
pumpkins into coaches,
and mice into horses,
lowness into loftiness,
and nothing into everything'
—Percy Bysshe Shelley

A chance meeting of Cinderella and
the Happy Wanderer under a South
African mulberry tree.

Vive le Group

Ever since the French Revolution *fraternité* has had a special meaning for the children of France. It appears in its purest spirit in the yard of a Grenoble *lycée* (left) But variations can be found over a community comic book in Rouen (right), where five friends study their favourite strip, anxious to act out the next instalment. In its feminine form *fraternité* tends to become a clique whose main function, the internationally childish game of character assassination, is practised by three French girls on their way home from school.

Clubs are to include someone out

Self-imposed segregation. Boys are
pointedly excluded from a round of
feminine chat in a Yugoslavian
village.

An Englishman's tree house is his
castle, especially if no girls are
allowed to domesticate it.

All brides are beautiful

The bride wore a petticoat and her mum's old shoes. Her train was of antique net curtain, and she carried a bridal bouquet of plastic roses. The maid of honour wore a ski-sweater and a hank of fox fur, and the bridemaids were draped in contrasting costumes of sheet and bedspread.

And the wedding party all slid down the aisle.

Giant Step

Everyone today is aware that the teenager has become a new international class with its own dress, language and music, its own problems and passions. Babies and children under five have, for a long time, been a special group too—the favourites of psychologists who lead us to believe that if a child gets a proper start the rest of the run to adulthood will be relatively simple. But the boy in shorts and the girl with plaits, at left, belong in a strange, uneasy category: neither children nor teenagers, they stand on the borderline between the two.

In the following essay the well-known novelist Colin MacInnes suggests that this period of pre-adolescence is little discussed and seldom written about, because it is so painful that the mind protectively chooses not to remember. He nevertheless approaches these thin-skinned years by bravely summoning up his own pre-adolescence in Australia, remembering how totally uneasy he felt in any company.

As observed in this article and reflected in the collection of pictures which follow, the pre-adolescent period is tricky and hard to define. To bridge over this awkward age one Indian tribe in Brazil's Mato Grosso area take the horrendous measure of placing young girls, just at puberty, in a special hut and keeping them hidden away for a year (p. 264) until they have taken the giant step into what the tribe considers the full state of womanhood. Biologically, of course, the coming of puberty should put children definitively in the realm of adolescence. But this definite physical maturity does not always free them from the feeling that, when they behave like little children, they are somehow letting down the side, or, when they act like adults and adolescents, they are ridiculous imposters.

Through the looking glass to adolescence

Colin MacInnes

Adults have vivid memories of childhood, and no less vivid of their adolescence when they falteringly grew into men and women. For me the brief period between these two, that moment when the young human creature is neither child nor nubile, remains plunged in the deepest recesses of our memories, as if we wished to hide these recollections from ourselves. Can this be because they were so painful—and yet so splendidly entrancing? Do we forget them because this was, in some sense, the most vital moment of our lives, and thus one we dare not fully remember because the sense of their loss would be so poignant?

How can we recover this feeling of *pre-adolescence* when we looked askance suddenly at children, whom we had thought hitherto to be our comrades, and also at older boys and girls whom we had thought to be our admired mentors and protectors? That feeling of the year in which we rejected the games and prattle of our juniors, and suddenly gazed fearfully at our seniors, whose mysterious codes and conduct we knew we should shortly have to try to understand? Perhaps the best way for an adult to recapture that trembling, golden moment, is to remember himself, or herself, when in love. For between the two states—adult passion and amorous pre-adolescent agony—there are striking similarities. In both, life is *heightened*—its temperature electrically rises—so that prior existence seems drab and lifeless by comparison. Yet in both, the heart is also exposed to searing pains from which, in more normal conditions, it is cushioned or immune. At the end of childhood, or in adult passion, the spirit soars to rare vivid delights, and yet is horribly vulnerable to misery.

Since no attempt to recall the farewell to childhood can be other than subjective, may I first offer the reader the bare facts of my own pre-adolescent condition. My mother, after divorcing my father (for the best of reasons), had re-married an Australian—or, more properly, a Tasmanian, since the latter do not like to be called the former, even though they are. I was thus, at the age of five, transported to Australia, where I was reared, till the age of nearly seventeen, in Hobart, Melbourne and, during long school holidays, on the sheep stations and fruit farms of the all-embracing bush. My mother, whom I never loved (I have always, for this reason, found the Oedipus complex difficult to credit), though I certainly feared her, conducted herself, in this colonial décor, like a suave settler in darkest Africa. Beneath a torrid sun, and often in circumstances of great material distress, she resolutely maintained the values—and the accent—of her Kensingtonian culture in London, much to the astonishment of the natives. Yet curiously, she got away with it: she was so resolute in her rejection of everything Australian (except for the beaches, for she loved swimming) that she acquired the reputation of a 'character', or 'card', and made countless Australian friends who almost wept when she finally departed.

My step-father, the Tasmanian, was an extroverted engineer, brilliant at technology, hopeless in business, tough, generous, kindly and totally devoid of the faculties of speculative thought or of imagination. It cannot be easy for any man—and especially one not reflective—to see every day, in his step-child, the living proof that some other man has earlier occupied his wife's bed; and though he acted justly to me, there was no point of human contact whatsoever. I do not think he hated me, but simply wished that I was not there at all.

The reader may imagine that this is the prelude to the artist's habitual tale of an unhappy childhood. But quite on the contrary. I loved Australia, I loved (dreadful admission!) my school, I loved my mates, the sea, the bush, the sun, and that ingrained Australian habit of granting independence early to their children, giving them responsibilities beyond their years, and letting them fight, roam, dream, make idiots of themselves without too severe a retribution. If my mother irked me, as she constantly did, I took her swimming and swam further out than she could. If my step-father shanghaied me to mow the lawn or clean his car, I vanished with my pals till we all returned at night for the ritual flogging. Youth has such energy, and in Australia such licence, that its elders fight a perpetually losing battle.

I first became aware of adolescence when my elder brother entered that estate. Hitherto, though he was a year and a half my senior, we had played and fought together in games and battles ferocious and intense. He had once tried to kill me with an axe while I defended myself with a hastily snatched dustbin lid. On the other hand, we had ridden miles together in the eucalyptus-sodden country, on bicycles or horses, and swum in creeks, dams and gorgeous bays, singing in parts to each other and enacting fantasies of bushrangers or explorers. But suddenly all that stopped. My brother's friends became attentive to their dress, bought razors, and instead of hitting or teasing me as before, treated me with an aloof, tolerant condescension. They stole whisky from my step-father's demijohn in the tool-shed, smoked pipes and cigarettes behind the woodpile, and chased me away when I tried to partake in any of these mysteries—the more so after, in all innocence, I had entered my brother's room to find them engaged in competitive masturbation, a sight which—in the brief glimpse I was vouchsafed of it—filled me with mingled terror, envy and fascination.

Then my brother began chasing *girls*. They phoned: he phoned. He stole my step-father's car on several occasions and they drove off, before my puzzled spying eyes, in the direction of the beach. Letters arrived which he seized from my hand, when I fetched the mail, and hid. He wrote poems, and when I found and laughed at them, he scarcely deigned to beat me. Soon it became apparent some great change had happened to him which removed him, for the moment, from my society. He shared jokes with my step-father that I did not understand—and was chased from the room if I tried to. Exchanges became minimal, except when he wanted me to lend him a tie, a tennis racquet, or mysteriously vacate my room for an afternoon and not come back till tea time.

Worse befell when my own favourite mate Jack was also thus suddenly transformed. When young males reach puberty, there are savage re-groupings of old friendships, and those to whom the miracle has not yet occurred are cast out by their dearest comrades who ruthlessly seek new friends

Three ten-year-old Spanish boys, dressed in their national costume, strike manly poses on a street corner of Fuenterravia during a local festival.

among older boys. The rejected feel like neophytes who have—all unjustly—been refused access to the temple. They experience deep pain and indignation—and yet are haunted by the feeling that they in truth do not merit the privilege of belonging to the inner circle which these erstwhile comrades have abruptly entered in confidence and glory.

I cannot speak of England or the United States, but in Australia most boys and girls know what physical changes are involved in adolescence—or, at any rate, know about these in theory. Among animals—for even city dwellers make off in summer to the bush—it is all there to be observed, conversation about humans is extremely frank, and when youth sleeps out on the beaches in the hot seasons, it is all there clearly to be seen (and heard). Yet to know what 'happens' is not at all to know what the sensation is. And thus, as the child enters the brief pre-adolescent stage, there come moments of decisive revelation in which, if physical adulthood is not actually achieved, it can at any rate be more realistically imagined.

Up on the river Murray, there is a garden area of the state of Victoria where fruit is grown in endless acres with row upon row of plums, apricots and peaches extending over hill and dale for miles. On an orchard where I used to go for holidays I met, in the fruit-gathering season, a half-caste aboriginal of indeed repellent aspect, who was much taunted by the white pickers both because of the innocence of his race, his bizarre English, and his air of dumb docility—which hid in fact, however, a considerable fund of guile. Fruit-picking is exhausting work, as you climb on the ladders in the broiling sun, a huge canvas bag suspended tugging on your neck and banging awkwardly upon your belly, stretching amid spiky foliage to pluck the hot ripe fruit—of whose taste your gluttony is soon disgusted, so that these delicious globes and ovals soon seem nauseous. Since the pay is by quantity, not time, you must struggle on—and here the aboriginal had come into his own, for while the white pickers often subsided for brew-ups of billy tea during their numerous 'smoke-ohs', the aboriginal toiled on, his centuries of habit enabling him to do without rest or water.

Since I was not paid for picking, being a guest of the orchard-owner and a boy, and since the men pickers had no use for me but to light fires for their tea, I used to wander off and help the aboriginal. At first I was scared of him, for his bent, millennial features seemed forbidding, and his age-old melancholy eyes were so remote as to seem utterly indifferent.

Besides, he looked grubby and unkempt, and seemed to confirm all the tales I had been told of the aboriginal delight in a diet of worms and lizards, of their fecklessness, dishonesty, and sudden treacherous malice. Yet I was attracted to him as much by the fact that he accepted my company without surprise, as by the affection I felt suddenly for the first adolescent I had known who, while having manifestly crossed the perilous threshold into early manhood, did not seem to reject, as my brother and his friends had done, any lad like myself who had not yet achieved that transformation. He also shared his cigarettes without condescension and a leer, and as I, hitherto, had only smoked surreptitiously cooking herbs wrapped in lavatory paper, the extension of this privilege delighted me.

When the evening came, and the fruit was weighed, and the pickers made off to their tents beside the farm to drink and gamble, the aboriginal lingered after them and beckoned me. Lowering his eyes, then gazing at me with a crafty smile, he asked if I'd like to come down to the river for a swim. As I hesitated, both because I knew my hosts would certainly object ('You can't trust the abo, son'), and because truth to tell I was still frightened of him, he reached out one hand and, with a gentle plucking gesture, tugged reassuringly at my shirt. I looked round at the house, nodded quickly, then whispered I'd meet him down by the cow tracks to the river. He set off ahead whistling, with that jaunty barefoot aboriginal prowl, while I, making a prudent détour round the milking sheds, caught up with him among the ferns and reeds that bordered the clayey windings of the Murray.

Here he immediately undressed, and plopped into the river like a porpoise. I followed timidly and, when I swam out, could no longer find him. Searching somewhat anxiously in the gathering gloom, I suddenly felt myself heaved up out of the water on his shoulders, tossed upwards like a pancake, and dropped with a whack on my back: whereupon he leaped on top of me so that I sank some feet and surfaced breathless in a rage. Seeing I was alarmed, he smiled, trod water in front of me, wiped the hair out of my eyes and patted me gently on the cheeks. Then he laughed, beckoned with a dark lanky arm, and swam slowly to the shore, turning sometimes to make sure I was following.

There, while we had a cigarette, he gazed at me craftily, then rose and, to my great surprise, stood knee-deep in the stream and bedaubed his whole body with its ochred mud. As soon as it had partly hardened, he began to trace patterns on his body which I recognized, from photographs I had seen, as being those appropriate to an initiation. He stood proudly before me in the rising moonlight, flashed his teeth grinning, then advanced, pulled me to my feet, and led me to the water. There he anointed me fondly with the slime, told me to lie down, and traced similar patterns on both sides of my body. While he did this, he examined me minutely, his hands wandering promiscuously, familiarly, but without violation. As I lay next to this boy-man by the river, I felt an exaltation—he was promising me that the strength he possessed would soon be mine as well. I reached up and kissed his muddy face, but he laughed, rose briskly to his feet, dived in the stream and disappeared towards the further shore.

At home, my first pre-adolescent encounter with a girl was with Oenone—incredibly so called, but she once told me her mother was fond of poetry. Hitherto girls, who once had been companions, had become, as adolescence approached, a scourge and enemy. The former tomboys had been transformed, as they reached their early teens, into dreadful little ladies, moving in defensive, disdainful groups, and darting quelling sarcasms at any boys of their own age who approached them. For this seems to be the only period when the warfare between the sexes becomes so acute that the rival armies will not even engage in battle.

Oenone was about seventeen, and she used to work two hours in the evening tidying up, for such limited help was all my mother could afford. Because she considered me a boy, I had become her intimate in the kitchen, though to my elder brother her attitude was much more aloof and cautious. She regaled me with tales of the 'boys' who took her dancing at the Bambalina Cabaret—a local dance-hall, as I imagine it now, as innocuous as could be, but seeming by her account the height of wickedness and glamour.

About this time, though as yet no untoward hair had appeared upon my body, I had joined the school cadet corps, which had a dazzling uniform like that worn by Latin American officers. When first I wore this, the sight of my youthful body in the mirror convinced me I was now a *man* and, trembling with daring, I invited Oenone, after I'd helped her with the washing-up, to come and gather fruit with me in the back garden. She smiled to herself, then laughed and agreed, and we made for the hammock that was strung, beneath the Southern Cross, between a peach tree and a nectarine. Reaching up for fruit, and being flung together by the extreme discomfort of the hammock, I began to fondle her, at which she giggled, slapped me, but didn't stop me. ('Hands off the model, son' she said. And 'Don't try anything I might forgive, but couldn't forget.') Even if I had known what to do, and even if I had been capable of doing it, I believe Oenone's prudence, if not virtue, would have halted my endeavours; but as it was, I had a melancholy gnawing sense of inadequacy. Clearly, I no longer felt towards her as a boy—the uniform no doubt encouraging this sensation—but equally, I was as yet unable to act towards her as a man. Sensing this, she was indulgent, and yet slightly mocking: I realized with a pang she did not feel I was dangerous, yet also with excitement that she felt I might become so before long.

For now I had reached the condition I am trying to evoke: that of being suspended between two states of being, not quite belonging to either, and fluctuating almost hourly between excessive reversion to childhood, and impossible demands that a manly status should already be conceded to me. The chief characteristic I remember of this brief period is its sudden swings between extremes of morbid gloom and inexplicable ecstasy. At one moment I would set off for long walks besotted with rapture, singing Schubert to the stars. At the next, I would sit on the woodpile in solitude convinced that I was cut off from all my past, and that all futures were barred to me irrevocably. My comrades having passed this state, or not yet having reached it, I found that the supports of old friendships were suddenly withdrawn. Out of a deep instinct to protect my state of isolation, I became a prodigious liar and thief, and failed in critical school examinations. My parents (who, like so many parents, must have forgotten that they, too, had once passed through this miserable condition) adopted a censorious attitude which made matters, if that were possible, worse. I tried to take refuge in consoling arts appropriate to my condition, and read ecstatic Keats and looked at glowing reproductions of Botticelli: but art, alas, though it certainly explains life and enhances it, is of no help to those whose own grip on life is insecure, and the dreams of the poets and painters only reinforced my gloom.

At this time I also became entangled with religion. I had never been baptized into any faith, and attended a school where religious instruction was minimal and formal, yet now I began to contemplate infinite things. I did not of course then understand what part of this impulse was genuine, and what larger part of it emotive and unreal, as I sat out services in church and read holy works seeking for impossible consolations. What I sought, but did not know it, were love and reassurance: but on a lad in this condition these are almost impossible to bestow except, perhaps, by some older person of infinite comprehension and wisdom, and such I was not then lucky enough to find.

I was also afflicted by curious snobberies. I began telling all my friends (who were not in the least bit interested) that I was not *Australian*, but *English*—hoping thereby to create, in the emotional void that enfolded me, the impression that I belonged to a suaver, surer world. I took to visiting, in my one good suit, older friends of my mother's and sought to impress them by the brilliant maturity of my uncouth observations. I affected, to mask the inner doubt and emptiness, an attitude of nonchalant indifference to all whom I encountered—a tactic which failed completely to impress the matter-of-fact Australians, though it no doubt irritated and surprised them.

But then the pendulum would swing upward to the skies, and life would become more beautiful than it had ever been before—and, I believe, than it would ever again be in the future. I have said how attached I was to my Presbyterian school, and at this time it took on an unexpected glamour. The masters seemed benevolent and full of consideration for my pretensions, the sportsmen young heroes out of legends, my comrades worthy companions before whom my undoubted gifts might shine. Even the buildings and the grounds seemed beautiful. The latter in fact *were*, for the astute Scottish worthies who had founded the academy had purchased a vast tract of land on the confluence of the river Yarra and a stream called Gardiner's creek. And though the sham red-brick Gothic of the school was in reality hideous, it seemed glorious to me, and I wandered among the gums along the river in the evening, long after I should have returned home, watching the oarsmen and the swimmers, and feeling part of a splendid and devoted confraternity of like-minded young.

The reader must please not laugh if I recall that, at this critical time, I was also protected by the mantle of Lord Baden-Powell. The scout troop to which I belonged was a tough and enterprising one. We often set out for the bush at night, pulling a trek-cart laden with scouty gear far out into the country. How beautiful the wild, untutored, hot, untidy Australian bush can be, so unlike the laundered countrysides of Europe, so welcoming, by its very indifference, to a fervent youthful spirit! We camped and swam and sang and built trestle bridges and cooked truly revolting food around fires whose smoke chased the myriads of mosquitoes. Most fortunately, this troop was not over-burdened with Powell-esque ideology and, forgetting the ten scout laws (or most of them), we indulged to the full in a brash outdoor hedonism which was the perfect antidote to urban gloom.

Thanks to the more pretentious of my mother's friends, I was also, at long last, able to meet girls on a footing that released me both from their venom and, if they were older than I was, from my painful feeling of animal inadequacy. For one of these older ladies was mad about theatricals and, since I was a cute kid and a show-off (Australian, 'skite'), I shone on these occasions—or at any rate, thought I did sufficiently to give me the courage, or effrontery, to talk to these girls without fear of their claws or, worse, indifference. I began to conceive passions for some of the older of them and wrote them facetious-romantic letters to which they were often kind or indulgent enough to reply. Masking my tremors, I even became the confidant of some of my brother's sirens, who sometimes kissed me surreptitiously, filling me with shock, ardour, and frustration.

My sister died when she was still a baby, and I have always regretted I had only brothers. For however much a man may later grow to understand women—if that is ever fully possible—I believe the daily company of the other sex must be a chief key to knowing them. I have tried, in a novel (*June in her Spring* of 1952) to describe the feelings of a girl poised on puberty, and women have been good enough to say June is convincing (and not just a young boy transposed into a girl). Yet since I had no sister to observe, and since, at this time, I had not yet loved a woman who could tell me, I must try to describe young girls as I saw them in the same stage of pre-puberty as my own.

I think they were *wiser* than we were. It is not only that boys mature later, generally, than girls do, but that the girls seemed closer to reality than we: to understanding what is possible, and what not, in human life at any juncture. With adults, among the many things which differentiate the sexes, it seems to me that women do not *boast* nor *fuss* as much as men. (As to the latter, try nursing a sick man or woman, and see the difference! As to the former, it may be the physical transformation that men must achieve in sex which accounts for their anxious vainglory.) Yet even with young girls, this greater female poise is evident. This is not at all to deny passion, wildness, fervour to such girls: but these seem to come when there is a pretext for them, not just when self-induced for the mere sake of sensation without reason. Even before puberty, a girl seems to guess what being a woman will mean for her in the near future, while boys more often carry

their boyhood into early manhood.

They are *kinder* than we are. Boys are barbarians, moving in irrational killer groups, fickle in feeling, vain and resentful. Girls have their mean, spiky nastiness, it is true, yet they seem more humane. Dangerous in flocks, they seemed gentler and sweeter than boys of that age were when you could catch them alone a moment.

The physical changes that come to boys as they approach puberty are, heaven knows, disturbing, but the far greater shock to girls must be horribly disturbing. The erotic reverie of the boy may be alarming, yet on the whole agreeable; the comparable change in a girl's body cannot but be unpleasant, despite the promise that it holds out—once this is kindly and truthfully explained to her—of later glory and fecundity. I remember a moment when this sharp change overtook a girl while we were gathering shrimps on an Australian beach. Far out on the rocks, beneath the huge sky of Western Port, we were chasing them in warm limpid pools, the picture of juvenile amity, when suddenly she stared at me in white alarm and fled off ashore to her mother without a word. An aunt, to explain her conduct, later told me she had had a distressing and mysterious experience. Boys joke about this, and they are little horrors to do so. For on girls it must lie

heavily, though perhaps (like pregnancies and the menopause later) these are cardinal events that give to women their greater sense of reality, even if these hard reminders of our animal nature may deprive them of the man's greater faculty to brood and dream.

As both sexes near the threshold of adolescence, they are, despite their tribulations, suddenly blessed with qualities that childhood had denied them. The chief of these, I think, is that they are able, overnight almost—and to the great astonishment of their elders—to accept untoward *responsibilities*. To see a boy of this age, or a girl, suddenly take charge of a situation—often to avert an impending disaster to a younger child—is a touching sight. In the child one suddenly sees the embryo adult, hitherto thought to be too young, who can now confidently handle problems believed to be beyond its nature.

Most parents, it seems, are not very useful at this period. It is, of course, confusing for elders not to know if their off-spring are infants or adolescents, yet there does often seem to be a failure of adult empathy. The battles of pre-adolescence must almost always be fought out alone. (Perhaps, since in the last resort we always *are* alone, nature is wise to make us pass the hard test in solitude so early.) It also seems that our social order is so designed that maximum demands are made at this moment of minimum capacity to meet them—examinations, in particular, and an insistence on right social behaviour ('You're no longer a child') at a time when the psyche is most raw and unprotected. Much is said today about the difficulties of teenagers, but by comparison with this earlier state, their trials seem to be negligible; for sixteen and seventeen are not just three or four years older than thirteen and fourteen but, psychologically speaking, almost a generation more. (I have often, incidentally, wondered at the aplomb with which African children of both sexes pass this difficult stage. Perhaps their greater poise and maturity are due to that ferocious blend of animal love and family cohesion that marks their upbringing. Also, no doubt, to the fact that educational demands, at this age, are not so severe as in Europe on the young boy and girl . . . though doubtless, with Independence and nationalism, they will soon become so.)

Some readers may feel that I have exaggerated the particular wonder of this pre-adolescent moment; and might say that childhood itself, or first adolescent love, or marriage, or childbirth, are more critical moments in our lifetimes. I do not think so. Romeo and Juliet, the archetypal lovers of our language, stood briefly at this threshold of their short lives, and in no other play has Shakespeare given to human love so unbearable an intensity. May is beautiful, but surely late March or April are more poignant. At all events, looking back as best I am able over half a century, I can think of no moment in my life which, once it had so quickly passed, left me with such a sense of loss.

Also with hindsight, I wonder what could have been done to make the transition easier and more bearable. Perhaps parents can't do much more than just to recognize what is happening to their children, and to bear with it, so that one chief pressure, of parental disapproval, is removed. In the end though, I think, all that their elders can really offer to the young is food and security, which means love and tolerance.

If children at this age could receive more sexual enlightenment than, even today, they do, this would help them enormously. It has always seemed to me strange that we instruct the young carefully and as truthfully as we can in everything except this—and leave it to them to pick up vital knowledge as best they can and often inaccurately, to say the least. What kids of this age need I feel are plain, unadorned facts: to be told simply what *happens*, what to avoid in sex and how to make sex into love. It seems to me monstrous that girls, in particular, are exposed to the perils of puberty without being told precisely how unwanted pregnancies can be avoided. How severely they are blamed when these occur! But are we not also to be greatly blamed for leaving them in an ignorance we would never allow if it were a question of their health in general? Moral and social considerations are of course important, and it is surely right to present them, but what growing children also need is straight, unloaded information.

Obviously, too, our educational system weighs far too heavily on the pre-adolescent young. I recall that although I left school with all the necessary scholarships to go to university, I decided (at the tender age of fifteen, and much to my parents' horror) not to do so, since I knew the anxieties of exams had nearly wrecked me. An instinct for self-preservation prompted me to take a job rather than walk the treadmill of examinations for a further spell of university years. Of course I lost by this as a scholar, but I also survived psychologically as I believe I would not have done had I been processed in the examination machinery much longer. This may be a subjective experience: more stalwart—or more insensitive—children may perhaps take the pressure of examinations in their stride, without hurt to their natures. But because I believe educational demands, at this age, are often far too severe, I think that we should consider giving embryo adolescents a total holiday from intellectual pressure lasting at least six months or a year. Does it really matter that they will temporarily fall behind other boys and girls in the race for certificates, degrees and jobs? It seems probable, to me at least, that any child so treated and allowed to work at his own rhythm will catch up later on, when young men and women in their early twenties so often wilt because of the hot-house pressures applied too fiercely ten years before. In pre-adolescence, not only the body but the mind as well are preparing for their great adventure: the overwhelming onslaught upon a burgeoning mind of many possibilities, and the feeling of bewilderment which invades the eager, anxious, inquiring youthful brain. At this moment, the child, soon to be one no longer, should, at best, read, see and hear anything created that its own spirit yearns for and, at the same time, be able to relax in physical enjoyment of a swiftly growing body. In our blindly competitive society, we are so terrified of sloth that we cannot understand the value of healing leisure.

Can there be any serious doubt that adults might learn enormously about this life if they could bend an attentive and patient ear to what the young say and do at this critical age? From our contemporaries we certainly gain most of our illuminations. But these come from people of like experience to our own, even though their knowledge may be more profound than ours. From the vivid incoherence of children we can also learn, get insights of a different order from voices rising, as it were, from the infancy of the human race. But if we listen to boys and girls at the very moment when they may seem most pimply, awkward and disagreeable, we can partly penetrate a mystery most of us once felt heavily within us, and have now forgotten. This mystery is the very process of creation of man and woman: at first, that of our birth, about which we consciously remember nothing, and then, as we stand at pre-adolescence, on the threshold of our adult lives, a change that amounts almost to rebirth and is the moment of greatest *instinctive* self-awareness in our lifetime—even if, while it is happening to us, we have not yet achieved our highest level of conscious understanding.

Christ spoke to the elders in the temple when he was twelve years old; and what is more, the elders had the good sense to listen to him. I see nothing 'miraculous' in this fable, but an allegory, like so many in the gospels, of human experience and wisdom. The mission and the trials lay ahead for him in adolescence and in manhood; but at this moment when he was neither boy nor man, he spoke with the innocent assurance that belonged to his young and illumined years.

Catching tiddlers in an English stream near Canterbury.

Coming of age

It is a well-known fact that girls begin to mature more quickly than boys. Even before the real physical changes of puberty occur, girls in many parts of the world are expected to act as grown women, sometimes even to marry when they are still children.

Berber girls of Marrakesh (right) have a relatively easy time of it. At puberty they put on the silver coins that are the traditional festive jewellery of womanhood, but they go without the veils which their Arab sisters must wear. The putting on of women's dress—whether bangles and beads or high heels and lipstick —is an initiation into womanhood practised nearly everywhere.

More unusual is the rite practised by the Camaiura Indians in Brazil's Mato Grosso. At the beginning of puberty, the girls are separated from the rest of the tribe and then put away in a hut for an entire year. At the end of this period of initiation they will dance, accompanied by men playing long musical pipes, in a final ceremony marking their arrival into the full state of womanhood. The girls at left are pale-skinned compared to their accompanists, because they have been allowed to emerge from their confinement only for rehearsals like this one.

Initiation into life

In most primitive societies, a boy is not a man until he has endured the dramatic rites of initiation. In some places he must sacrifice some of his teeth, or some of his blood, stand in the heat and smoke of a fire or walk over hot coals. In Arnhem Land, Northern Australia, the aborigines practise circumcision, a ritual that can take anywhere from three weeks to five months. The boy suffering the application of symbolic paint (below) is about nine years old.

A more festive ritual, which is practised by the aborigines all over Australia, is the corroboree. Primarily a dance, it is nevertheless intended to be a deeply significant event.

Youngsters who learn the ways of the corroboree are supposed to be learning the secrets of life. The boy at right, however, faces these mysteries with grinning irreverence—even though the tree of life grows symbolically from his navel.

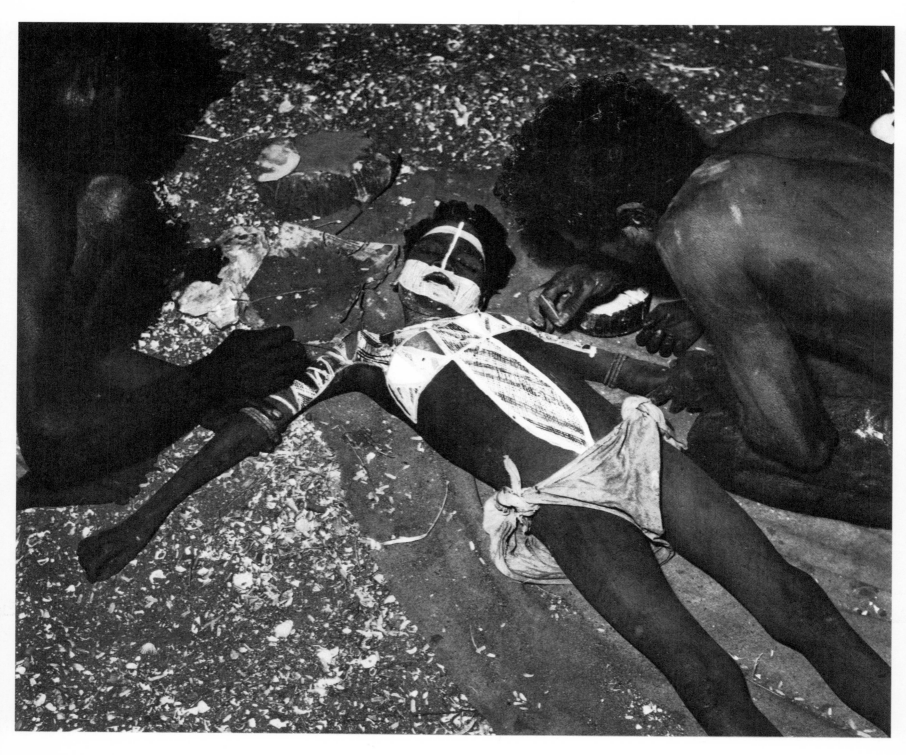

Creating the image

Every little girl wants to grow up to be a beautiful woman. These girls of the Yoruba Tribe of Western Nigeria are only about ten years old, but they are already capable of matching their poise, if not their figures, against the tribe's most venerated models of feminine beauty.

Once a year, during the Festival of Images, statues from all the shrines of the village of Ilobu are carried into the central market place—not to be worshipped as gods, but to be honoured for their beauty. Carrying the statues is also an honour, and the young girl at left bears her distinguished burden with pride.

The girl on the right is a member of the royal family of Idanre, as signified by her coral necklace. Her mannered pose is as carefully and deliberately sculpted as the sacred carved pillar which supports the royal verandah.

269

The unease of in-between

Two shrouded figures move against a background of old Islamic architecture, shrinking from the photographer as they do from any contact with the outside world. They are both young girls of Kasvin, Iran, where Islam is orthodox and girls are veiled from puberty.

In sharp contrast is the appearance of a French girl of the same age. There is no formal marking of her entrance into adolescence—only a slight awkwardness, likely to be magnified under the maternal gaze.

In Lapland, where reindeer are herded like cattle, two brothers get their rope on a stag.

Boys of the Dominican Republic master the machine, a primitive press for extracting juice from sugar cane.

Doing a man's job

Autumn leaves provide agreeable employment for two American boys on a Saturday afternoon.

In Panama City, business enterprise means shaving ice for cold drinks to be sold to hot Americans.

A woman's place

In many parts of the world it is still necessary for children to share the responsibility of making the family living. The barefoot girl at right is doing more than woman's work, cutting sugar cane alongside her father in the mountains of Colombia.

The little girl at left, however, is only playing at work in an Italian field. She is too young and too well-off to know what real labour is, but the pose is symbolic. Work, whether real or not, implies maturity.

Cheers and tears

The 'civilized' world has its own peculiar community rituals and informal puberty rites which provide outlets for all kinds of adolescent steam. Fans of all ages and sexes exercise their vocal chords at a football match (Arsenal vs Liverpool) but fainting and screaming at the appearance of an idolized pop group (in this case, the Pretty Things) seems to be an activity exclusive to girls between the ages of twelve and sixteen.

Pop and Pennywhistle

Even before toys are finally put away there is a budding of new interests that prove to be even more fun.

Skilfully foiling a tackler, an American tomboy shows her friends how to play football.

Because the Queen has awarded the Beatles the Most Excellent Order of the British Empire, the fans create a Most Excellent Din at the gates of Buckingham Palace.

The Kwela, a type of music peculiar to South Africa, is the spontaneous togetherness of penny-whistles.

278

Messing around

They have outgrown the playground
but not the play,
They want to be just kids,
but couples, too.

Pairing off

Hungary: First dance produces self-conscious giggles but genuine pleasure, as well.

England: Finals of the 'Dance News' festival for under-twelves provides the very young with a self-conscious chance at elegant precosity.

France: Formality is definitely a thing of the past for a teen-age couple outside a cinema.

New Hampshire

Children's voices in the orchard
Between the blossom- and the fruit-time:
Golden head, crimson head,
Between the green tip and the root.
Black wing, brown wing, hover over;
Twenty years and the spring is over;
To-day grieves, to-morrow grieves,
Cover me over, light-in-leaves;
Golden head, black wing,
Cling, swing,
Spring, sing,
Swing up into the apple-tree.

T. S. Eliot

Bibliography

The World of Children

Ariès, Philippe. *Centuries of Childhood*
Benjamin, Z. *The Young Child and his Parents*
Bühler, C. *From Birth to Maturity*
Gesell, A. and Ilg, F. L. *The Child from Five to Ten*
Hostler, P. *The Child's World*
Hunnicutt, C. W. *Answering Children's Questions*
Ilg, F. L. and Ames, L. B. *Child Behaviour*
Jersild, A. T. *Child Psychology*
Lane, Homer. *Talks to Parents and Teachers*
Lady Longford. *Points for Parents*
Mead, Margaret and Wolfenstein, M. *Childhood in Contemporary Cultures*
Reeves, Marjorie. *Growing up in Modern Society*
Strang, Ruth M. *An Introduction to Child Study*
Tudor-Hart, B. *Learning to Live*

Beginnings

Bowlby, J. and Fry, Margaret. *Child Care and the Growth of Love*
Chukovsky, Kornei. *From Two to Five*
Estvan, F. and E. *The Child's World; his Social Perception*
Fletcher, Ronald. *The Family*
Gesell, A. *The First Five Years of Life*
Isaacs, Susan. *The Nursery Years*
Isaacs, Susan. *Social Development in Young Children*
Winnicott, D. W. *The Child and the Family*
Winnicott, D. W. *The Child and the Outside World*
Ziman, E. *Jealousy in Children*

Learning

Ashton-Warner, Sylvia. *Teacher*
Christianson, Helen M., Rogers, Mary M., and Ludlum, Blanche A. *The Nursery School: Adventure in Living and Learning*
Frank, M. and L. K. *How to help your Child in School*
Hollamby, Lilian. *Young Children Living and Learning*
Hourd, Marjorie C. *Some Emotional Aspects of Learning*
Hymes, James L. *Before the Child Reads*
Isaacs, Susan. *The Children We Teach*
Isaacs, Susan. *Intellectual Growth in Young Children*
Marshall, Sybil. *An Experiment in Education*
May, Dorothy E. *Children in the Nursery School*
Mitchell, Lucy Sprague (ed.) *Know Your Children in School*
Moustakas, Clark E. and Berson, Minnie P. *The Young Child in School*
Neill, A. S. *Summerhill: A Radical Approach to Education*
Piaget, Jean. *The Language and Thought of the Child*
University of London Institute of Education. *Studies in Education*
University of London Institute of Education. *First Years in School*
University of London Institute of Education. *Aspects of children's development from the ages of 4 to 7.*

Playing

Callois, Roger. *Man, Play and Games*
Hartley, R. E., Frank, L. K. and Goldenson, K. M. *Understanding Children's Play*
Jackson, L. and Todd, K. M. *Child Treatment and the Therapy of Play*
Lowenfeld, M. *Play in Childhood*
Matterson, E. M. *Play with a Purpose for Under-Sevens*
Opie, I. and P. *The Lore and Language of Schoolchildren*
Radler, Don H. and Kephart, Newell C. *Success Through Play*
Schwartz, Alvin. *A Parent's Guide to Children's Play and Recreation*
Tudor-Hart, B. *Toys, Play and Discipline in Childhood*

Exploration

Chaloner, L. *Questions Children Ask*
Murphy, Lois Barclay and others. *The Widening World of Childhood*

Fear and Wonder

Chaloner, L. *Feeling and Perception in Young Children*
Griffiths, R. *Imagination in Early Childhood*
Jersild, A. T. and Holmes, F. B. *Children's Fears*
Piaget, Jean. *Play, Dreams and Imitation in Childhood*

The Hostile World

Bettelheim, Bruno. *Truants from Life*
Collis, A. and Poole, V. E. *These our Children*
Ford, Donald. *The Deprived Child and the Community*
Frank, Anne. *The Diary of Anne Frank*
Kuchler-Silverman, Lena. *My 100 Children*
Lewis, H. *Deprived Children*

The Shaping Spirit

Isaacs, Nathan. *The Growth of Understanding in the Young Child*
Jersild, A. T. *In Search of Self*
Piaget, Jean. *The Child's Conception of the World*
Piaget, Jean. *The Moral Judgement of the Child*

Giant Step

Coleman, James S. *The Adolescent Society*
Farnham, Marynia F. *The Adolescent*
Gallagher, J. Roswell and Harris, Herbert I. *Emotional Problems of Adolescents*
Hadfield, J. A. *Childhood and Adolescence*
Jordan, G. W. and Fisher, E. M. *Self-Portrait of Youth*
Mays, J. B. *The Young Pretenders*

Publishers' Acknowledgements

The publishers wish to express grateful thanks to the following for kind permission to reproduce quotations in this publication:

Jonathan Cape Ltd, London: *The Fisherman's Food* by Drummond and Wilbraham

The Clarendon Press, Oxford: *The Allegory of Love* by C. S. Lewis

William Collins, London, and Random House Inc, New York: *Memories, Dreams, Reflections* by C. J. Jung, translated by Richard and Clara Winston

Faber and Faber Ltd, London, and Harcourt, Brace & World Inc, New York: from 'Animula' and 'New Hampshire', *Collected Poems 1909–1962* by T. S. Eliot

Sigmund Freud Copyrights Ltd, Mr James Strachey, Hogarth Press Ltd, London, and Liveright Publishing Corporation, New York: 'Beyond the Pleasure Principle', Volume VIII (1920–1922) of the Standard Edition of *The Complete Psychological Works of Sigmund Freud*

Victor Gollancz Ltd, London, and Alfred A. Knopf Inc, New York: *Darkness and Day* by Ivy Compton-Burnett

Michael Joseph Ltd, London: *Roads to Ruin* by E. S. Turner

Oxford University Press, London: 'White Snow' from *The Owl in the Tree* by Anthony Thwaite

Routledge & Kegan Paul Ltd, London: from 'What is Man?', *Between Man and Man* by Martin Buber

Mr Richard Sadlier: *Fanny by Gaslight* by Michael Sadlier